# The Veil of Depiction

## Painting in Sufism and Phenomenology

Evrim Emir-Sayers

PICT Books

Paris Institute for Critical Thinking

PICT Books

Halman Library

The Halman Library, inspired by the life and work of Talât Sait
Halman (1931-2014), is an imprint of PICT Books dedicated to the
Ottoman Empire as well as its temporal and spatial horizons.

Published by the Paris Institute for Critical Thinking (PICT)

www.parisinstitute.org

ISBN: 978-2-494635-03-6

"We must understand why what one culture produces has meaning
for another culture even if it is not its original meaning."

*– Maurice Merleau-Ponty*

# Contents

## Introduction

Miniature painting is one of the finest art forms to emerge from the Middle East. Flourishing from the 14<sup>th</sup> to the 19<sup>th</sup> century in the Timurid, Safavid, and Ottoman empires, this art had loftier goals than the mere production of aesthetically pleasing images. Informed by the mystical tradition of Sufism and drawing on philosophical concepts pioneered by thinkers like Muhyiddin Ibn Arabi (1165-1240) and Jalaladdin Rumi (1207-73), miniature painting aimed at nothing less than a transformative manifestation of the absolute. Western artistic preoccupations such as verisimilitude were irrelevant; materials and techniques were devoted to the goal of divine self-revelation through art.

Ultimately, the art of miniature painting succumbed to Western encroachment. Heavily dependent on court patronage and cultural sophistication, the art form could not survive the 19<sup>th</sup>-century dissolution of the political structures and cultural codes that formed its foundation. But ironically, the art's obsolescence in the Middle East was followed by its "discovery" in the West. Featured in early 20<sup>th</sup>-century expositions in Paris and Munich, miniature paintings started influencing artists such as Henri Matisse and the Fauves, precisely at the time when Western painting was breaking away from its emphasis on verisimilitude and seeking inspiration in alternative artistic approaches from around the world.

The Western artists who appropriated the formal features of miniature painting were not familiar with the art form's mystical and philosophical underpinnings. Nonetheless, their paintings spawned philosophical readings of their own, particularly in phenomenology, where they inspired thinkers such as Martin Heidegger and Maurice Merleau-Ponty to formulate a new philosophy of art. Uncannily, these philosophers'

1

ideas often bore striking resemblance to the Sufi philosophical framework of miniature painting. The Middle Eastern idea of "life-giving" art, for instance, was mirrored in the Heideggerian understanding of "art as unconcealment."

The connection between Sufism, miniature art, and modern Western painting was first highlighted in the seminal work of Michael Barry. However, no study to date has traced the line of transference from Sufi philosophy to miniature painting, miniature painting to 20th-century Western art, and 20th-century Western art to phenomenology. Further, no study (not even within Sufism) has systematically mapped Sufi philosophy onto miniature art, and there has been no comparative analysis of the two philosophical traditions, Sufi and phenomenological, that stand at the beginning and end of the line of transference. Here, I aim to address these issues by demonstrating both the historical continuity and the philosophical common ground of the "Eastern" and "Western" traditions in question.

My goal is not to demonstrate some direct or indirect indebtedness of modern Western philosophy to Sufi thinkers. Rather, I intend to uncover the theoretical and practical compatibility of Sufi and phenomenological approaches to art. I believe that we can combine these approaches to achieve innovative readings of "Eastern" and "Western" art alike—in particular, we can avail ourselves of phenomenology to arrive at readings of Middle Eastern miniature painting that are unprecedentedly nuanced while at the same time true to the original philosophical underpinnings of the art.

Chapter 1, "Miniature Painting in the Middle East," will focus on three 16th-century authors from the Middle East who concerned themselves closely with miniature art: Dust Mohammad, Qadi Ahmad, and Mustafa Ali. As these authors will show us, the history of Middle Eastern miniature painting is, at the same time, the history of the court milieus in which this intricate and elite form of art was produced. Artists' careers waxed and waned with the fortunes of their noble patrons, ranging from the Mongol Ilkhans to the Mughals in India. Patronage was fickle, however, and depended on a religious zeitgeist which often turned hostile to figurative art, branding it as a blasphemous imitation of divine creative activity.

It was this fickle zeitgeist that gave the pragmatic impetus for the alliance between Sufism and miniature art, an alliance we will begin to explore in Chapter 2, "Artists and Sufis." To offer a religious *apologia* for the suspect and endangered art form, our Middle Eastern authors establish a parallel between the mystical path of the Sufi and the artistic path of the miniaturist, describing the miniaturist and the Sufi as seekers of the same truth. The perceptual apprehension of the absolute, which the Sufi pursued through philosophical contemplation and a variety of mystical practices, is said to be pursued by the miniaturist through his art.

Building on this parallel between artist and Sufi, our authors trace the outlines of a philosophical argument for viewing the miniature painting itself as a privileged locus for the self-manifestation of the absolute. Far from being developed systematically, this argument is based on frequently interspersed allusions to various aspects of Sufi philosophy, allusions that are impossible to interpret without a basic understanding of this philosophy. To enable such an understanding, Chapter 3, "Ibn Arabi's Ontology," will be devoted to *The Bezels of Wisdom*, a treatise by the philosopher Muhyiddin Ibn Arabi, widely regarded as one of the most accomplished exponents of Sufi thought.

Ibn Arabi views the world of particulars as the self-manifestation of the absolute to itself, without which the self-knowledge of the absolute would remain incomplete. This leads the philosopher to reject a duality between the absolute and the manifest, such as exists between the concepts of a "creator god" and such a god's "creation." Instead, Ibn Arabi postulates an interdependency between the absolute and the manifest, or the uncreated and the created, in which neither side enjoys an ontological, hierarchical, or temporal primacy over the other.

Human beings play a privileged role in the absolute's self-manifestation by acting as mirrors in and through which the absolute can perceive itself. However, since the self-manifestation of the absolute always takes the shape of a simultaneous self-disclosure and self-concealment, ordinary perception is incapable of apprehending it fully. Human beings must "polish" themselves as mirrors, i.e., purify themselves from the clichés of their ordinary perception, to open themselves to the perception of the absolute. Also, there are some particularly suitable vehicles for the contemplation of the absolute, among which Ibn Arabi names the female countenance. But even if the desired perception is achieved, the experience remains indescribable by the Sufi, whose outlandish utterances can easily leave him misunderstood as a heretic or madman.

Chapter 4, "Sufism and Miniature Painting," will trace how Dust Mohammad, Qadi Ahmad, and Mustafa Ali employ Sufi ontology to explain miniature art. Even when a painting seems to represent an ordinary thing from the world of particulars, such as a rock or a river, our authors maintain that the painting can unlock perceptual dimensions not opened up by the thing itself. Thereby, the painting enables viewers to perceive the simultaneous self-concealment and self-disclosure of the absolute as described by Ibn Arabi. In other words, our authors view miniature painting as a similarly privileged locus for the self-manifestation of the absolute as the female countenance highlighted by Ibn Arabi.

4

Chapter 5, "The Journey to the West," will outline the introduction of Middle Eastern miniature painting to Western audiences and artists in the early 20th century. This transfer occurred in the context of Western imperialist expansion, a process that often involved the dissolution of the courtly milieus that kept miniature art alive, the absorption of bound miniature albums into Western collections, and the dismemberment of these albums with the goal of marketing individual miniature paintings at auctions and exhibitions. While the result of this historical process was the disintegration of miniature painting as an art form, it was also through this process that the technical vocabulary of the art form was appropriated by 20th-century Western painters.

It is worth repeating that these artists, foremost among them Henri Matisse, were unaware of the Sufi ontology accompanying the techniques they adopted. All the more remarkable, then, that in the Middle East and the West alike, these techniques were employed to enable a form of perception not given by the contemplation of mere things. In both cases, we find an understanding that painting is not a mere stand-in, a more or less verisimilitudinous copy of a thing that readily discloses itself to ordinary perception, but a locus and device for the unlocking of perceptual possibilities beyond the quotidian. While 21st-century Western scholarship is only just beginning to catch up with the Sufi dimension of miniature art, artists such as Matisse managed to intuitively grasp its deeper intent.

Inspired by modern art, Western philosophy also began to engage with painting as a challenge to ordinary perception conditioned by our everyday presuppositions, and as an enabler of a more primordial form of perception. Chapter 6, "Phenomenology and Art: Balzac, Husserl, Heidegger," takes us from "The Unknown Masterpiece" (1831), a short story in which Honoré de Balzac invents the figure of Frenhofer, possibly the first modern painter in history, to "The Origin of the Work of Art" (1935-36), a treatise in which Martin Heidegger argues that a painting by Vincent van Gogh reveals its subject—a worn-out pair of shoes—in a way the presence of the actual shoes would be unable to accomplish.

Heidegger's thoughts on art must be viewed in the context of his broader philosophical project, which rejects the dualistic ontology encompassing most of Western philosophy from Plato to Descartes. Simplistically expressed, this ontology performs a division between essence and existence, postulating that a pure, unattainable essence precedes and provides the ontological ground for all that is in existence. This division paves the way for a number of other dichotomies, such as God and creation, body and soul, and subject and object, which, to Heidegger—just as to Ibn Arabi—cloud an authentic form of perception that would reveal to us an underlying and primordial unity free of these artificial categories that separate the human being from her existential envelopment.

However, to both Heidegger and Ibn Arabi, the matter is not as simple as replacing a Platonic (or Cartesian) duality with some undifferentiated notion of unity. Just as Ibn Arabi holds that the self-unveiling of the absolute is also, at the same time, a self-veiling, Heidegger regards the process of being as the simultaneous occurrence, or "strife," of what he terms "the self-concealing earth" and the "self-unconcealing world." It is this strife that causes our incomplete perception, an incompletion that in turn makes us falsely assume a dichotomy. Turning to Van Gogh, Heidegger argues that the painting acts as a locus in which the processes of self-concealment and self-unconcealment not only take place but are also held in tension for the viewer to experience, a claim that echoes our Middle Eastern authors' views on miniature painting as a locus for the self-manifestation of the absolute.

Chapter 7, "The Artist as Phenomenologist: Merleau-Ponty and Cézanne," explores the philosophy of art proposed by Maurice Merleau-Ponty, who builds on the work of Heidegger to investigate how exactly the work of painting—as both verb and noun—occurs. How does the painter perceive, how does she process this perception, and how is the perception, in turn, translated into a work of art? What is the relation between the artwork and that which was originally perceived by the painter? And how does the work go on to engender a new kind of perception in its beholder?

In his seminal essays, "Cézanne's Doubt" (1945) and "Eye and Mind" (1961), Merleau-Ponty develops concepts such as the "narcissism of perception," in which a network of perceptual reciprocity covers itself over all perceiving and perceived things to constitute a field of absolute perception, and devotes extensive attention to various painterly techniques such as the employment of color. Merleau-Ponty's work both reinforces the philosophical bridge I aim to build between phenomenology and Sufism, and equips us with a phenomenological toolkit that complements the understanding of miniature painting supplied by Sufi philosophy. Where Sufi thought gives us the broad ontological outlines of how the art of painting fits in with the self-manifestation of the absolute, Merleau-Ponty helps us concretely imagine how the miniature painter and the individual miniature painting may act as conduits for this self-manifestation.

I wish to reiterate at this point that I am not claiming a transmission of ideas from Sufi thought to phenomenology via miniature painting and modern Western art. Rather, I aim to highlight a parallel between two philosophical approaches that dissolve a static, dualistic understanding of being and replace it not with a simple monism, but with a complex interweaving of concealment and unconcealment, veiling and unveiling, invisible and visible. Intriguingly, both approaches single out painting as a locus for this interweaving and as a means through which the beholder's perception may be enabled to apprehend it. The most direct connection between the two approaches lies in the transmission of certain key techniques from miniature to Western art, techniques that were employed by both sides to undermine, expand, and recondition the beholder's everyday perception of the world.

Further, I am not offering a critique of Sufi or phenomenological approaches to art. My aim is not to analyze whether any one of these approaches is logically consistent, philosophically convincing, or experientially verifiable. While I will lay out the tenets of each approach and explore how they may be brought into dialogue, I will not delve into possible or actual criticisms of these approaches as philosophical systems of thought. Finally, whenever I attempt such a dialogue, it is not in the belief that the two sides are saying the same thing. I merely claim that the approaches are sufficiently similar to enable, on a practical level, their combined application to works of art in general and miniature painting in particular.

The conclusion, "Towards a Phenomenology of Miniature Painting," demonstrates this claim by applying the Heideggerian concept of the "great work of art" to Middle Eastern illuminated manuscripts, and then exploring two particular miniature paintings by the master Kamaluddin Bihzad (ca. 1450-1535) in a way that combines Sufi philosophy and Merleau-Pontian phenomenology. These brief explorations will showcase that Sufism and phenomenology can, indeed, be combined in approaching art and that, in combination, they bring us within touching distance of an exceptional form of art often assumed to be historically, philosophically, and culturally out of reach.

## 1. Miniature Painting in the Middle East

### *Introducing the Sources*

From the Mongol Ilkhanate (ca. 1256-1353) to the Indian Mughal Empire (ca. 1526-1857), a set of highly sophisticated court milieus came into being around a succession of Muslim rulers. Their shared language was Persian, which emerged as the *lingua franca* of the cultural and political elite in the non-Arabic realms of Islam from the Bosphorus to the Ganges.[1] In these court milieus, artists, writers, and mystics came together to create a unique melting pot of ideas and techniques.[2] One of the most remarkable expressions of this "Persianized" cultural world was the art of miniature painting.

Our exploration of miniature painting will be guided by three sources from the 16th century, namely Dust Mohammad's preface to the Bahram Mirza Album (1544), Qadi Ahmad's *Gulistan-i Hunar* (Rose Garden of Art, 1596-97), and Mustafa Ali's *Menakib-i Hunerveran* (Epic Deeds of Artists, 1587). These texts—the first two from the Safavid and the latter from the Ottoman Empire—are widely viewed as the most important primary sources on this art available to us today.[3]

The Bahram Mirza Album, an exquisite compilation of calligraphy and miniature paintings, was commissioned by the eponymous Bahram Mirza (1517-49), younger brother of the Safavid ruler Tahmasp I (r. 1524-76). Around 1544, Bahram Mirza charged Dust Mohammad of Gawashwan (1531-64), a courtier and calligrapher, with the compilation of the album. In Dust Mohammad's words, it was his lord's desire that:

> the scattered folios of past and present masters should be brought out of the region of dispersal into the realm of collectedness. In this regard the exalted command and sublime order was issued to this poor slave,

miserable speck of dust, distracted sinner, Dost-Muhammad the Scribe.[4]

Dust Mohammad's preface to this album, which offers a brief but enlightening history of calligraphy and miniature painting as well as assessments of various artists working during the author's own time, is the oldest extant Middle Eastern primary source featuring a systematic account of the miniature tradition.[5]

Our second Safavid author, Qadi Ahmad of Qum (dates unknown; last recorded date 1606), served as vizier to Ibrahim Mirza (1543-77), son of the abovementioned Bahram Mirza. While his main task at Ibrahim Mirza's court consisted of preparing and registering official documents,[6] Qadi Ahmad was also a writer and intellectual who authored various works of historiography and literature. And even though he was not a professional calligrapher or artist,[7] he penned the *Rose Garden of Art*, an entire volume on the history and practice of calligraphy, miniature painting, and other arts of the book.[8] Qadi Ahmad confidently describes this volume as "a treatise [...] which may find a place in the flourishing *kitab-khana* [library] of the Shah of the World and the Khan of the Time, by the side of masters of writing and artists."[9]

Finally, our third primary source stems from Mustafa Ali of Gallipoli (1541-1600), one of the most prominent historians of the Ottoman Empire. The first treatise on art by an Ottoman author, *Epic Deeds of Artists* became very popular and was copied out numerous times over the centuries, with some manuscripts owned by Ottoman sultans and high officials.[10] Mustafa Ali had enjoyed training in calligraphy and was an occasional patron of the arts, commissioning six miniature paintings for a copy of his *Nusretname* (Book of Victories), presented to Sultan Murad III ca. 1583. The sultan enjoyed the work enough to order a new, royal edition, for which forty-eight miniatures were produced in the royal studio, with Mustafa Ali himself supervising the whole effort. This project, occupying the better part of a year, provided Mustafa Ali with much of the expertise underlying his *Epic Deeds of Artists*.[11]

Compared to the works of Dust Mohammad and Qadi Ahmad, *Epic Deeds of Artists* is quite a worldly book, one that frankly discusses matters such as exorbitant prices, forgeries, and frauds in the Ottoman art world. In Esra Akın-Kıvanç's words, "Ali's main motivation in composing the *Epic Deeds* was to enlighten the collectors and to inform the ruler and the powerful statesmen from an insider's perspective of what was really taking place in the art world under their very eyes."[12]

All three texts are examples of the literary genre of *tadhkira*,[13] albeit, in the case of Dust Muhammad's Preface, in somewhat rudimentary form. A *tadhkira* is a biographical compendium that presents the eminent personages in a given field—for instance saints, poets, civil servants, or artists—in chronological, and partly mythologized, succession from the origins of the field to the present day. Composed in prose with interspersed pieces of poetry, *tadhkiras* contain information on the history of the field, its major schools and styles, its main practitioners, and contemporary developments.

Like most genres of court literature, the *tadhkira* was highly formalized. Akın-Kıvanç points out that authors used "manuals intended for epistolary compositions containing quotations from Qur'anic verses, *hadith*, and sayings of saints and sages"[14] in order to flesh out their accounts or provide examples reinforcing their points. She also offers a good summary of the literary techniques employed by *tadhkira* writers:

In order to reinforce an idea, for example, they used poetry, metaphor, and allegory; cited previous authors who wrote on the same subject; told folk stories and anecdotes; or quoted Qur'anic excerpts and the Prophet Muhammad's traditions [*hadith*] in Arabic as uncontestable sources of authority. Writers often sought to establish unbroken and legitimate lines of historical achievement on a given subject by mentioning historical events and prominent figures as a backdrop to contemporary achievements. Finally, references to first-hand observations about people and events under discussion were another means through which *tadhkira* authors strove for increased credibility.[15]

It should be clear from the above that these are not texts on the philosophy of art, or even the history of art, as the terms would be understood today.[16] In addition, Qadi Ahmad and Mustafa Ali devote the bulk of their chapters to calligraphy, only turning to the other arts of the book, including not only miniature painting but also arts such as decoupage, gilding, and book binding, in the final chapter of their respective works. Almost no individual artwork is mentioned, let alone analyzed in detail; techniques such as the usage of color or perspective are not discussed; and no systematic criteria are established for judging artistic quality. Nonetheless, as we will see, the works offer invaluable insights into the art of miniature painting as well as its historical and philosophical connotations.

## The Album as a Work of Art

Any assessment of Middle Eastern miniature painting must start with the recognition that such paintings were rarely intended as stand-alone works of art. Rather, as in the example of the Bahram Mirza Album, they were generally commissioned or compiled as parts of bound manuscripts. Often, such manuscripts were devoted to versified mythological tales, such as Fariduddin Attar's

13

*Canticle of the Birds*, that served as allegories for Sufi thought, with scenes that were crucial to the plot and the allegory illustrated by miniature paintings.[17] And even if a manuscript was a compilation of miniature paintings intended to exhibit the most outstanding exemplars of an era, school, or culture, the overall artistic and philosophical intent of the book was not abandoned. Qadi Ahmad's poetic description of a compilation album commissioned by Ibrahim Mirza demonstrates this unity of intent:

> Its beautiful pictures were of such a degree that
> From the point of view of cleanness and distinction
> Nothing but the soul would find a place in it.
> Because of the images of flowers and shapes of birds
> It was a Paradise unspoiled by the autumn wind.
> Thousands of its roses and tulips, stems and petals,
> Were immune from the harm of storms and hail.
> Youths represented with sunlike faces, in shame,
> Had closed their lips in their conversation.
> All of them united in war and peace,
> Not like the dwellers of the world full of hypocrisy and dishonor!
> Day and night companions of the same quarters,
> Men devoid of discord in their communion![18]

The production of such an album, especially when commissioned by a royal patron, was a multi-faceted, time-consuming, and expensive project: one need only remember the year it took the Ottoman royal studio to produce a version of Mustafa Ali's *Book of Victories* for the Sultan's library. Qadi Ahmad describes the creation process of Ibrahim Mirza's compilation album as follows:

> In Holy Mashhad he put together an album (*muraqqa*) of the writings of masters and paintings of Maulana Behzad and others. It was completed with the help of rare masters, skillful craftsmen,

incomparable experts in writing, and peerless calligraphers. Indeed, such an arrangement was made and such an album showed its face, that every page of it was worthy of a hundred praises, nay every specimen of it merited one hundred thousand lauds.[19]

To create albums of such distinction, a studio needed to include not only calligraphers and miniature painters, but craftsmen who measured, colored, and gilded the pages' margins; others who painted colorful ornaments for chapter headings and major passages; experts whose sole occupation was the collection and grinding of pigments to be used as color; specialists in the production of glues; artisans who worked with leather and lacquer to create book bindings; and binders who sewed the manuscripts together.[20] And, of course, the studio could only do its work thanks to the existence of complex supply chains spanning from India to Egypt and providing the various constituent materials of the manuscript from pigments to paper.

Obviously, such a "book" shares little but its name with the commodified object of mass production the average "book" has become today. These unique manuscripts possessed such extraordinary value that they were often exchanged as gifts between rulers. Looking at palace inventories of gifts presented to the Ottoman court, Akın-Kıvanç finds illustrated manuscripts of the *Shahnameh* and *Khamsa*, works by the Persian Sufi poet Nizami, "listed before such gifts as precious stones, silk, and various luxury items made of gold and ivory," and only surpassed in esteem by yet another book, the Quran itself.[21]

With such high value placed on the album as a material object, it should come as no surprise that "fake albums" were produced as well, for sale to wealthy dabblers in art who were not knowledgeable enough to recognize the genuine article. Following Mustafa Ali, Akın-Kıvanç is careful to distinguish the album as an integral work of art from such "mix-and-match albums" that "destroyed not only the form but also the meaning of what once was art.".[22]

Albums were as fragile as they were precious, and as their owners' fortunes faded, the albums themselves could meet tragic fates. No example illustrates this better than the end of the Ibrahim Mirza Album as retold by Qadi Ahmad. When political rivalries led to the killing of Ibrahim Mirza by poison, his wife Gauhar Sultan (1540-77) resolved to destroy the album rather than see it fall into the hands of her late husband's enemies. And so, she "washed out the album with water, although no one had seen a similar one and its price was tantamount to the *kharaj* (tax income) of a whole clime.".[23]

However, the final, lethal blow to the album as an integral work of art was dealt in the late 19th and early 20th century, when many albums ended up in the hands of Western art speculators who dismembered and sold them page by page, a practice that Michael Barry has aptly described as a "profitable artistic massacre.".[24] To this day, many such pages are exhibited as individual "works of art" in museums around the world.

## Patronage

As should be clear by now, the art of miniature painting was inextricably connected to royal patronage or, at the very least, the munificence of prestigious and wealthy elites. For reasons I will discuss in detail below, religious patronage was not an option,[25] and there was no question of the art surviving and thriving in the hands of talented and motivated but poor and badly networked individual painters. Mustafa Ali sums up the importance of court patronage as follows:

> Let it not be hidden that, [among] artists and men of refinement, the pursuit of skill in their arts, the concentrated striving to increase their capabilities, the gradual emergence of perfected talent, and the serious

expenditure of fruitful time and full commitment to hard work is facilitated through either the favor of rulers of abundant munificence or the unrestrained support of exalted viziers.[26]

Artists were not the only ones dependent on court patronage— the same held true for the authors of our sources as well. All three of them were courtiers, and they wrote not for the sake of producing knowledge, but for the pleasure of their courtly sponsors. This is especially clear in the case of Mustafa Ali, whose often bluntly critical writings made it difficult for him to obtain a reliable source of patronage, presenting a life-long impediment to his ambitions and career. Many of Mustafa Ali's works, including *Epic Deeds of Artists*, were written for potential patrons in hopes of obtaining their favor.[27] It is well worth remembering this dependence on patronage, and the consequent desire to please patrons, when assessing our sources' take on issues such as miniature art and Sufi philosophy.

## Court Milieus

It was in the 15th and 16th century, at the courts of Timurid, Safavid, and Ottoman rulers, that the art of miniature painting arguably experienced its golden age. The Timurid court, with its patronage of the arts, was often idealized by later writers such as Mustafa Ali[28] as the prototype of a royal artistic milieu:

> During the reign of Prince Baysunghur Khan [ca. 1397-1433], it was decided to preserve people from [spiritual] impoverishment by encouraging true poetry, by making calligraphers delight in beautiful writing, and through the consummate benevolence of the ruler, by bestowing the highest ranks and offices upon men of perfection. It is even accounted that, in his prosperous time, forty talented calligraphers in his service gathered in a school and paradise-like workshop, a joyous place famed like heaven, which would make a picture gallery envious.[29]

Baysunghur's capital of Herat[30] played an important role in the transition of political rule over the Persian heartlands from the Timurid (ca. 1370-1507) to the Safavid (ca. 1501-1736) dynasty. The city, which retained significant prestige as a provincial capital under the Safavids, served as a trans-imperially recognized political and cultural center, preserving artistic traditions, schools, and individual masters of Timurid origin and transmitting them to the new Safavid rulers. Its role in the course of Islamic art has been compared by Michael Barry to that of "Florence, in the same age, in the evolution of Western art."[31]

Under the early Safavids, miniature painting reached its zenith in terms of excellence, official recognition, and prestige.[32] The most outstanding patrons of the art were the first two Safavid shahs, Ismail I (r. 1502-24) and Tahmasp I (r. 1524-76), as well as Bahram Mirza (1517-49), Ismail's son and Tahmasp's younger brother, and Ibrahim Mirza (1543-77), Bahram's son. Ibrahim Mirza, who established his own court milieu in the provincial capital of Mashhad, was eulogized as follows by Qadi Ahmad:

> No sultan or *khaqan* possessed a more flourishing library than that powerful prince. The majority of excellent calligraphers, painters, artists, gilders, and bookbinders were employed there. [....] Some 3,000 volumes and treatises were collected in the library of that light of every eye.[33]

Remarkably, many Timurid and Safavid rulers were not only patrons but also practitioners of the arts, including miniature art itself. Both Qadi Ahmad and Mustafa Ali reserve the highest praise for the artistry of Tahmasp and Ibrahim Mirza, with Qadi Ahmad calling the former an "incomparable master rising above all artists in drawing and painting"[34] and describing the latter as having "golden hands in painting and decorating; he achieved great success because of his refinement of thought and deep meditation."[35]

While the Safavid courts allowed miniature art to flourish in unprecedented ways, they also showcase the drawbacks of the art's precarious dependence on royal sponsorship. The stories of Tahmasp and Ibrahim Mirza in particular illustrate what could become of artistic milieus when patronage came to an end due to a ruler's displeasure or demise. Tahmasp abandoned his interest in the arts around 1544-45, eventually going so far as to ban the non-religious arts in Persia altogether.[36] After his death in 1576, his nephew and protégé Ibrahim Mirza became embroiled in political intrigue and, as mentioned above, died by poison the following year. His studio was dispersed, and many priceless artworks destroyed.

Turning to the Ottoman Empire, we see that miniature painting flourished, with brief exceptions, from Mehmed II to Mehmed III (1451-1603). Shortly after the conquest of Constantinople in 1453, the Ottomans had already established court patronage for calligraphy and miniature art,[37] and by the late 16th century, this patronage was resulting in masterpieces such as the *Siyer-i Nebi* (Life of the Prophet), commissioned by Murad III (r. 1574-95), completed under Mehmed III (r. 1595-1603), and containing over eight hundred illustrative miniature paintings of exceptional artistic quality.[38]

Having conquered Constantinople, Mehmed II (r. 1451-81) also invited Western painters to his court. We know of at least eight such artists, including Gentile Bellini, to whom the portrait of Mehmed II now to be found in the National Gallery in London is often ascribed.[39] While not mentioning any of these names, Mustafa Ali nonetheless refers to one Ottoman painter influenced by Western masters:

Among the figural-painters of Rum, [there was] Musawwir Sinan Beg, who appeared at the paradise-resembling palace of Sultan Mehmed Khan, the conqueror of Constantinople [...]. He was a pupil of a Frankish master named Mastor Paoli, who flourished in Venice and became a most exalted artist in his field. And the said Paoli was an agreeable apprentice of a talented painter named Damian.[40]

This influx of Western artists, however, did not result in an adoption of Western techniques. A good example is the *Shema'ilname* (Book of Likenesses, completed before 1579), a compilation of physical descriptions and portraits of Ottoman sultans. The author, Seyyid Lokman (active 1569-95), and chief illustrator, Nakkash Osman (active 1560-92), did not have any direct evidence of what the sultans before their own times looked like. So, to guide them, David Roxburgh informs us, they used "a portrait series of the earlier sultans painted by European artists" as reference material.[41] However, the resulting portraits showed no recognizable Western artistic influence. The painters simply mined the European paintings for information regarding physiognomy and facial features, but embedded this input in the visual language of miniature art, avoiding "the European codes of optical naturalism: the use of modeling, chiaroscuro, a naturalistic palette, and perspective."[42]

## The Fortunes of Artists

Artists could use their proximity to the centers of power to establish careers as courtiers, bureaucrats, or political figures. Calligraphers had privileged access to such opportunities since they were often also employed as court scribes. Qadi Ahmad reports of one Qadi Abdullah of Khoy that his duties at the court of Tahmasp included composing "epistles in Turkish and Persian, which were sent to Rum [Rome, i.e., the Ottoman Empire] and the sultans of India."[43] And Mustafa Ali speaks of calligraphy as a highly marketable skill: "It is not easy for someone who has [mastered] calligraphy to possibly become so poor and needy. At the present time, there are calligraphers whose daily income is purses and purses of silver and gold.".[44]

While miniature painting did not necessarily come with the same career opportunities, certain painters were still able to attain positions of influence. Qadi Ahmad mentions Maulana Naziri of Qum, who, as Tahmasp's painting instructor, became "an intimate of the Shah.".[45] Dust Mohammad lists Amir Ruhullah, also known as Mirak Naqqash, who attained the post of royal librarian under the Timurid ruler Husayn Mirza Bayqara (r. 1469-1506).[46] And Mustafa Ali names Re'is Haydar, who, under Suleyman I (r. 1520-66) and Selim II (r. 1566-75), was the chief (*re'is*) of the Ottoman naval arsenal.[47] But even if no further posts were forthcoming, being a court miniaturist was no small privilege in itself, and Mustafa Ali maintains that miniature painters at the Ottoman court were both numerous and generously remunerated.[48]

However, as I mentioned above, court sponsorship also implied a constant element of precarity. Our sources describe the dissolution of one artistic milieu after the other, with its members dispersing throughout the Islamic lands in search of new sponsors. Conquerors could force artists to relocate, as in the example of Khwaja Abdul-Hayy, who was working in Baghdad when the city was sacked by Timur in 1401, and who spent the rest of his life in the Timurid capital of Samarkand.[49] Artistic centers could decline after conquest, as happened to the cities of Shiraz and Herat under Safavid rule, with artistic schools drying up and painters moving away over the course of one or two generations.[50] Artists could be forced to move as rulers changed their capitals, as in the case of the Safavid capital, which moved from Tabriz (1501-55) to Qazvin (1555-98) to Isfahan (1598-1736). Some artists negotiated the boundaries of empires, relocating with the waxing and waning of patronage among rulers on each side, as happened in the Ottoman-Safavid borderlands following the war of 1578-90.[51] And some cities, such as Safavid Qum, offered "a haven of refuge," in Boris Zakhoder's words, to "artists and master calligraphers who had been disappointed in life or who had had no success in court workshops and institutions."[52]

There were also many miniature artists who worked on a freelance basis in major or minor imperial centers. However, freelance painters' fortunes were even more precarious than those of their colleagues at court. They were dependent on one-off commissions from individual sponsors, such as Mustafa Ali himself, who, as mentioned above, ordered six miniature paintings for the first edition of his *Book of Victories* on his own budget.[53] Such freelance artists operated in a grey zone of legitimacy. Their lack of connection to an official workshop left them vulnerable to the charge of fraud, a charge levelled even by Mustafa Ali himself, who disparagingly remarked that "every new enthusiast painter" in Istanbul was keen to peddle the worthless sketches he had drawn "in the pitch-black of the night" to gullible art enthusiasts until not "even a rough sketch" was left in his portfolio.[54]

## 2. Artists and Sufis

### *Miniature Painting and Calligraphy*

The sword or the pen? Many Islamic bureaucracies rested on a fundamental distinction between military and civil services, with the military known as the *erbab-i seyf* (Men of the Sword) and the civil service known as the *erbab-i qalem* (Men of the Pen).[1] The distinction reinforces the perennial partnership—and rivalry—between sword and pen, not just as human instruments, but also as metonymies. Unsurprisingly, for our authors, pride of place belongs to the latter. Mustafa Ali makes the clearest argument here, maintaining that the pen's supremacy is "an obvious conclusion":

> First, in the [...] highest heaven and the supreme sphere, where the divine ordinance and secrets of faith arose, the Tablet and the Pen were present, while the firm sword was not. Second, it was at all times manifest that, in the hands of those who write, the sword was that which serves the pen. [These points,] I argue, brought the auspiciousness of the pen, and its consequent precedence [and] desirability from the darkness of sheer uncertainty out into the daylight of sound choice.[2]

At the outset of this passage, Mustafa Ali makes a metaphysical reference to a primordially existing Tablet and Pen serving as instruments of divine creation—a reference I shall explore further below. More important for our present purposes is that while the pen is positively contrasted with the sword, Mustafa Ali clearly associates the pen with writing—what he has in mind is not the miniaturist's, but the scribe's or calligrapher's pen.

Indeed, even the structure of our sources leaves no doubt that they privilege calligraphy over miniature painting. Dust Mohammad's preface is subdivided into seven main parts, of which three are devoted to writing and calligraphy, while two, each following a section on calligraphy, concern themselves with painting. When passing to the miniaturists, the author even excuses himself with the words, "since the writers have been mentioned in every chapter of this introduction, if I be so bold as to make mention of the artists, it may not be out of place."[3] Qadi Ahmad divides his treatise into four main chapters, the first three of which are fully devoted to calligraphy. Finally, of the five chapters in Mustafa Ali's work, the first four are reserved for calligraphy.

While calligraphy merits its own chapters, miniature painting is almost never treated on its own. One of Dust Mohammad's two sections on the art is devoted to "painters and limners";[4] Qadi Ahmad's final chapter is entitled "Conclusion: On the biographies of painters, gilders, masters of gold sprinkling and decoupage, dyers of paper, and bookbinders";[5] and Mustafa Ali divides his final chapter among "the sundry group of talented masters of decoupage, renowned figural-painters, and illuminators of discerning eye as well as limners of rare works, binders of artistry, gold sprinklers, rulers, and repairers of beautifully embellished works."[6] Clearly, then, miniature painting was regarded as merely one of many auxiliary arts that existed in calligraphy's orbit.

The interrelationship between the two arts also comes through in the careers of individual artists and artistic families. Amir Ruhullah, whom we encountered earlier as court librarian of Husayn Mirza, was a painter and calligrapher alike.[7] Similarly, Maulana Naziri of Qum was Shah Tahmasp's instructor in both calligraphy and painting.[8] And Matrakci Nasuh (ca. 1480-1564), one of the most famous Ottoman miniature painters, is listed by Mustafa Ali as the "inventor" of the *diwani* style of calligraphy.[9] Even where the arts of calligraphy and miniature painting did not coincide in the same artist, they were still closely interrelated. For instance, Rustam Ali, the nephew of the great miniature painter Kamaluddin Bihzad of Herat (ca. 1450-1535), was a renowned master of calligraphy.[10]

## The Religious Ambiguity of Painting

All these intersections notwithstanding, a dichotomy between calligraphy and painting can be sensed between the lines of our authors' accounts. In all three sources, calligraphy is glorified for its role in the transmission of the Quran and the sayings of the prophet Muhammad. And since writing is regarded as an indispensable component of religion, the art of writing is seen as a deeply religious—even pious—art. One searches in vain for such religious validation in the sections on miniature art, which, to the contrary, often sound apologetic—without quite pinpointing what the apology is supposed to be for.

We can reasonably connect this discomfort to the ambiguous attitude of Islamic cultures towards the depiction of living beings. As Zakhoder points out, the Quran itself "does not contain a forthright interdiction of making images of living beings. This prohibition [is] rooted in pre-Muslim conceptions."[11] But while the Quran itself may contain no "image ban," *hadiths*— anecdotes from Muhammad's life considered the second most authoritative religious source in Islam—contain quite explicit statements on the issue such as "every former of an image shall be in hellfire."[12] It was the religion's famous and uncompromising hostility to idol worship that rendered suspect, if not offensive, the production of any image that could potentially serve as an idol.

Nonetheless, we have seen that miniature art was widely practiced, and lavishly sponsored, in many Islamic contexts. This resulted in a tension between artistic tradition and religious suspicion that led to some fascinating artistic experiments, such as miniature paintings depicting the smashing of religious idols. Speaking of such paintings, David Roxburgh rightly comments that they "appear to risk the very practice that they depict."[13] A similarly paradoxical—and highly popular—artistic practice was figurative calligraphy, in which the totality of the written text takes on the shape of a living being. For a quotidian example, we can turn to Qadi Ahmad, who mentions an inscription that read "the price of sugar and candy has come down because of the sugar plantations," written in the form of "three or four men standing one under the other."[14]

Among the authors of our sources, the tension between religion and art is most explicit in Dust Mohammad, who claims that "by the externality of the religious law, the masters of depictation hang their heads in shame," before quickly adding that "portraiture is not without justification, and the portraitist's conscience need not be pricked by the thorn of despair."[15] Thus, Dust Muhammad confirms the religious disapproval of painting but also leaves the door open for a "justification" that may yet redeem the art.

While Dust Mohammad clearly states the existence of the tension, it is Qadi Ahmad who stages the most systematic attempt at its resolution. Earlier, we saw that Mustafa Ali regarded the sword as inferior to the pen—as long as it is in the service of writing. Qadi Ahmad divides the pen itself in two, with one—the reed pen—devoted to writing and the other—the animal-hair brush—to painting:

> The *qalam* [pen] is an artist and a painter.
> God created two kinds of *qalam*:
> The one, ravishing the soul, is from a plant
> And has become a sugarcane for the scribe;
> The other kind of *qalam* is from the animal,

And it has acquired its scattering of pearl from the fountain of life.
O painter of pictures which would have enticed Mani!
Thanks to you the days of talent have been adorned..[16]

The verses contain two references we will take up later: the association of the painter's brush with the fountain of life, which establishes a parallel between painting and divine creation; and a reference to the prophet Mani, which points to the relationship between painting and (ostensibly false) prophethood. For now, the most important point is that Qadi Ahmad describes the deity as creating the pen as both "plant" and "animal," thereby claiming the same religious legitimacy for painting as for calligraphy. In Zakhoder's words, "If, in the theological sense, the artist's brush has the same properties as the *qalam*-reed, then religious consecration applies to it as a matter of course.".[17]

## Calligraphers and Sufis

Zakhoder argues that Qadi Ahmad could only have made such a point in the context of a politically and culturally ascendant Sufism. What he has in mind is the Shiite school of Islam practiced and proselytized by the Safavid dynasty in Persia..[18] Safavid Shiism, he argues, "should be taken not only in its religious and political connotations, but also with that mystical and pantheistic content which was invariably associated with the Shia and which can be designated as 'Sufism.'" Khorasan, the province ruled by Qadi Ahmad's patron Ibrahim Mirza, was "an immense laboratory [in which] the Sufi-Shiite doctrine had been elaborated throughout many centuries,".[19] and it was here that miniature painting was able to step out of the shadow of calligraphy and acquire a religious legitimacy of its own.

In milieus that interlaced Sufism and art—and this included not only Safavid milieus, but also Ottoman ones which took their cultural cues from Persia—the figures of the artist and the Sufi started to overlap. Let us trace this phenomenon in calligraphy first, since the vast majority of examples given by our authors are calligraphers. Following this, we will check whether our observations are applicable to miniaturists as well.

Many calligraphers named by our authors were also Sufis. Qadi Ahmad talks of a master who was "a calligrapher, a scholar, a dervish following the right path".[20] and another who "became a devotee of Sufism.".[21] Mustafa Ali gives similar examples, showing that the artist-as-Sufi ideal passed over into Ottoman thinking as well. He mentions a calligrapher who was "a wayfarer on a praiseworthy path, a dervish of good disposition, a slave dedicated to writing, and a saint who bequeathed any and all good prayers and exalted favors that he received upon the poor of that region.".[22]

Some calligraphers in Mustafa Ali's account led ascetic lifestyles. Mawlana Qani'i, for instance, was "a dervish by nature and [a follower of] the commendable path [of mysticism]." The calligrapher "was content with dry bread and covetous [only] for a morsel. [And he was] satisfied with the provisions of ascetic abstinence and subsisted on barely enough to prevent the exit of the last spark of life.".[23]

Finally, certain calligraphers were disciples of prominent Sufis, such as the calligrapher Ali of Qain, who was "intoxicated with a sip from the goblet of Mawlana 'Abd al-Rahman Jami [1414-92], who sat at the heart of the gatherings of the intimates [i.e., Sufis] and who was the distinguished agent of divine truth at the meetings on law and religion." Mustafa Ali describes Ali of Qain as devoting his time to transcribing and copying Jami's poetic works, thereby rolling the practices of calligraphy and Sufi meditation into one.[24]

Mustafa Ali also conflates the master-disciple relationships central to the Sufi and artistic traditions, with the transmission of

Sufi insight becoming indistinguishable from that of artistic skill. Thus, one calligrapher "practiced writing under […] Mu'izz al-Din and became enlightened by savoring his teaching.".[25] Another, by the name of Abdullah Ashpaz, is described as "the shaykh of the copyists of Rum and the foremost spiritual guide of that group."[26] In fact, Mustafa Ali views the transmission of calligraphic skill as such a spiritual affair that even the physical presence of a master may not be necessary. Of a certain Mir Khubi, he maintains that "without seeing Sultan 'Ali of Mashhad in person, [but] acquiring from his tomb a reed pen that had been trimmed by him [and practicing with it] day and night, [Mir Khubi] learned from him."[27]

The example of Abdullah Ashpaz shows that Mustafa Ali viewed the totality of Ottoman calligraphers in a guild-like fashion, with the leader of the guild assuming vocational as well as spiritual functions. This understanding of the calligraphic tradition as a spiritually unified whole is reinforced by our Safavid sources Dust Mohammad and Qadi Ahmad. These cast Ali ibn Abi Talib (601-661), cousin of the prophet Muhammad and fourth leader of the Muslim community after Muhammad's death, as the "patron saint" of calligraphy. Both authors identify Ali as the inventor and greatest master of the Kufic script, the calligraphic style in which the Quran was first committed to writing. Ali becomes the originary figure of Islamic calligraphy as a whole, with all subsequent branches emanating from him..[28]

But the connection between Sufism and calligraphy went even deeper. To our authors, an artist's calligraphic skill was inseparable from their spiritual and moral qualities..[29] Mustafa Ali bluntly asserts that "A perfect person is necessary to discover a good calligraphic style,"[30] while Qadi Ahmad even calls on Plato to back up the point: "The sage Plato says: 'Writing is the geometry of the soul, and it manifests itself by means of the organs of the body.'".[31] The argument is clearly expressed in the following quatrain by a certain Maulana Sultan Ali Mashhadi, cited by Qadi Ahmad:

> The aim of Murtada 'Ali in writing
> Was (to reproduce) not merely speech, letters and dots,
> But fundamentals, purity and virtue
> For this reason he deigned to point to good writing.[32]

The further one progressed down the Sufi path, the higher one's artistic achievement was bound to be. This becomes clear in the following two excerpts from the "Epistle of Maulana Sultan Ali," again cited by Qadi Ahmad. In the first excerpt, Maulana Sultan Ali points to spiritual purification as a precondition of artistic success:

> Only he who of trickery, intrigues, and hypocrisy
> Has cleansed himself, has become master in writing.
> He who knows the soul, knows that
> Purity of writing proceeds from purity of heart.[33]

The second excerpt uses calligraphy as a metaphor for the path of spiritual purification:

> Like unto a *qalam* you will rub your head against the paper.
> Not resting a day or night from labor,
> Discard your desires,
> Turn away from the road of covetousness and greed,
> Wrestle with the cravings of the concupiscent soul.
> Then you will know what a minor religious war is.[34]

Progress, as both an artist and a Sufi, was ultimately seen as dependent on divine grace. The adept could practice sincere devotion and striving, but whether this would be rewarded with the hoped-for result was out of their hands. It is this logic that moves Mustafa Ali to statements such as "One thinks his penmanship is innate and his beautiful writing is purely God given" or "To [the] master, luminosity was handed down from the heavens.".[35] And since artistic merit was divinely bestowed, it could also be rescinded. Mustafa Ali relates the following anecdote about a certain Mawlana Mir Ali and his student, Mir Chalama:

Mir Chalama became such a leading figure and a rarity in lands far and wide that Mawlana Mir Ali guarded him and gave him permission to sign [...] in his name. [....] Yet, illbred and proud, [Mir Chalama] did not grasp the meaning [of his master's compliment]. And facing his master, he said, "Who do you think you are that I would prefer your signature?" [...] Mir Ali cursed Mir Chalama and, following his malediction, [Mir Chalama] was soon after blinded. The arrow of his teacher's appeal reached the [divine] station of favorable response..[36]

### Miniaturists and Sufis

Modern scholars have generally assumed that miniature art found itself "in an entirely different position".[37] with regard to notions of spiritual purity. Because of its implied connection to idolatry, so the going thesis, miniature art was inherently suspect and miniaturists guilty by association. Many anecdotes from our authors seem to back up this assumption, painting individual miniaturists in a less-than-favorable light. In a story related by Dust Mohammad, the miniaturist Amir Khalil causes his patron, Baysunghur Khan, bodily harm:

One night, in the company of His Highness, [Amir Khalil] began to joke, but the affair went so far that the heel of his boot unintentionally hit the prince on the forehead. His Highness's forehead was cut, and blood poured from his august head.

Aghast, the miniaturist flees the scene:

> Amir Khalil, wailing and lamenting, took flight to the chamber [...] and locked himself in. Having fled from the valley of boon companionship, he sat down in penitence..[38]

The story ends on a conciliatory note, with a display of generosity and forgiveness:

> The prince, [...] with all clemency and favor, came to the door of the chamber. Amir Khalil opened the door and fell at the feet of His Highness. The prince kissed him, took him back into the palace into the assembly and, showering him with favor and compassion, bestowed upon him all the silver and china vessels that were in use at the assembly, along with robes of honor of which Chosroes and Jamshid would have been proud. By showing him such generosity, [the prince] delivered him of his shame..[39]

The story seems to serve two purposes: on the one hand, it emphasizes the importance of patronage for the arts. On the other, it portrays the miniature artist as a transgressor—albeit in an oblique fashion, without tying his transgression directly to his art—while maintaining that his offense is, ultimately, unintentional and forgivable. It is the patron's duty, the moral seems to be, to protect the miniaturist in spite of his faults.

Another story of transgressive miniaturists, portraying the culprits even more negatively, is that of Abd al-Aziz, Ali Ashgar, and Shah Tahmasp. While the anecdote is found both in Qadi Ahmad and Mustafa Ali, it is the latter who elaborates most fully on the offense in question..[40] The miniaturists are introduced as:

> Khwaja Abd al-Aziz of Isfahan, a master of outstanding innovation who, moreover, tutored Shah Tahmasp in the art that is being discussed, and Monla Ali Ashgar, [the former's] recognized pupil and

a legend of the studio of the aforesaid shah. Though it was acknowledged that both of them were world masters, [...] they also had morals of similarly venomous quality..[41]

As in the previous story, the offense does not concern the art *per se.*

It is recounted that the aforesaid Shah Tahmasp had in his palace a handsome slave, Mirza Muhammad, son of Khwaja Qabahat, in whom he took delight and for whom he had affection. He was the shah's favorite and beloved. And during visits to his workshop, [the shah] always sat beside him. Now, the aforesaid Khwaja Abd al-Aziz and Ali Ashgar, conceiving in the valley of ungratefulness a series of stratagems and tricks, deceived the said Mirza Muhammad. United in hypocrisy and adding new distances to the edifice of separation, they left [the palace] behind and headed toward the darkness of India..[42]

Eventually, the three fugitives are caught and brought back to the palace. The ruler forgives his young favorite, but the miniaturists do not escape so lightly:

At first, in order to take revenge, [the shah] considered sentencing [...] the painters to death. But, since Khwaja Abd al-Aziz was his master and, with outstanding creations, a rarity among the decorative-painters, he refrained from executing him. [Instead the shah] gave [the two painters] a light punishment, severing with his own hands Abd al-Aziz's nose and Ali Ashgar's two ears..[43]

Like Dust Mohammad, Mustafa Ali concludes on a note of forgiveness, saying that Tahmasp eventually became "full of regret for having severed his master's nose" even though "the aforesaid painters had been extremely offensive and their deeds were utterly wicked." He closes his account with an admonition as to the proper conduct befitting a noble patron: "For men of high rank and position, [it is an act of] complete generosity and accomplished goodwill to choose discretion over imprudence at times of reckless fury and resentment.".[44]

Akın-Kıvanç reads this story as an expression of Mustafa Ali's "ambivalent feelings toward painters and the art of depiction.".[45] And it is true that our authors never depict calligraphers in such a negative way. If miniaturists could be men of such intemperance and loose morals, it seems, their art could not have been related to spiritual purity the way that calligraphy was. However, even if these anecdotes are read as an indictment of miniature art, it is a very indirect and oblique indictment indeed. The art itself is never at fault here; quite to the contrary, in Mustafa Ali's story, the main factor that saves Abd al-Aziz from being executed is his outstanding skill as a painter.

In fact, a closer look at our authors reveals that, at least in principle, the link between artistic and spiritual progress applied just as much to miniature art as to calligraphy. Let us return to Qadi Ahmad's poetic description of the Ibrahim Mirza Album which I cited in the previous chapter, and particularly focus on the following three lines:

Its beautiful pictures were of such a degree that
From the point of view of cleanness and distinction
Nothing but the soul would find a place in it.[46]

These lines make it clear that an outstanding miniature painting, just like outstanding calligraphy, was expected to manifest not just artistic beauty but also spiritual purity. Such purity could only be expressed in the painting if it also existed in the painter: above, we saw Qadi Ahmad describe his patron, Ibrahim Mirza, as possessing "golden hands in painting and decorating; he achieved great success because of his refinement of thought and deep meditation.".[47] And just as with calligraphy, a miniaturist's skill was only as great as their virtue. Mustafa Ali gives the example of the miniaturist Shah Quli Naqqash:

> Had he possessed morals as [excellent as] his art, Bihzad in his day could not have achieved the fame he did. And had he, in accordance with his conscientious nature, become a wayfarer on the path of divine observance, people would not in his time have talked about the art, reputation, and works of Mani.[48]

I will return to Bihzad and Mani as the archetypical painters below. Here, what is important to note is that, even in this negative appraisal by Mustafa Ali, painters are essentially held to the same standards as calligraphers. There is nothing inherently baser about miniature art than about calligraphy, and artistic and spiritual purity are equally connected in both arts. The fact that many individual miniaturists are portrayed as falling short of these ideals only confirms that the ideals applied to them.

Finally, let us turn to the issue of spiritual continuity and transmission. Our authors do not have much to say about the transmission of miniaturists' skill: unlike with calligraphy, there are no disciples of miniature art who become "enlightened" upon visiting great masters' graves. However, Dust Mohammad and Qadi Ahmad list Ali ibn Abi Talib as the "patron saint" not just of calligraphy, but of miniature painting as well. According to Qadi Ahmad, "the portraitists of the image of this wonderful skill trace this art to the marvelously writing *qalam* of [...] Ali."[49] And Dust Mohammad informs us that "the first person to adorn with painting and illumination the writing of the Word that is necessarily welcomed was the Prince of the Faithful and Leader of the Pious, the Conquering Lion of God [...] Ali ibn Abi Talib."[50] Here, Ali is positioned as the first writer and illustrator of the Quran alike.

## *Holistic Perfection*

What emerges from the above is that in Safavid and Ottoman high culture, the quest for spiritual perfection was seen as the bedrock of all other forms of personal advancement, and that the failure of this quest was seen as leading to a similar failure in other parts of one's life. The eminent Muslim scholar Abu Hamid al-Ghazali (1059-1111) expresses this idea succinctly with regards to artistic creation: "The essential beauty of man's creations such as poetry, painting, and architecture reflects the inner qualities of the poet, painter, and builder."[51] And Mustafa Ali reflects the same sentiment in the following thoughts on calligraphy and social advancement:

> Fine calligraphy is a virtue which unstintingly confers honor upon those who possess it. And the art of writing is a path toward nobility and fame, which leads those who command it to glory and high station, unless they are reproached by people for bad morals, or are notorious [for their] addiction to opium paste, opium or hashish.[52]

Underlying these thoughts is a holistic understanding of human perfection, with all aspects of human existence feeding back into all others. The possession of extraordinary artistic skill can only be one aspect or manifestation of this overall perfection. Even physical beauty is part of this package, as evident from Mustafa Ali's assessment of a particular calligrapher: "The beauty of his down, like the beauty of his writing, is a violet-colored [and] crisp legend of the gardens and meadows of his refined [nature]."[53]

Once again, this overall perfection finds its prototype in the figure of Ali ibn Abi Talib, who combines all the virtues an individual might hope to possess: "His Excellency Ali, on account of his efforts in calligraphy, his attainments in the Kufic hand that outshined others, his distinguished rank in the various sciences and virtues, and attainments in mysticism, is the chief of the saints and the foremost of the Imams of the Way of the Faith."[54] A warrior as well as a penman, Ali even transcends the original separation between pen and sword we observed at the outset of this chapter: "He is, in sum, the master of the sword and the pen. With him the saber and the reed pen are exalted."[55]

This holistic understanding of perfection, based on Sufi ideas, also explains the title of Mustafa Ali's treatise, *Menakib-i Hunerveran* (Epic Deeds of Artists). As Akın-Kıvanç explains, the Arabic word *manaqib* refers to deeds and character traits alike, implying "a focus on the subject's commendable actions as well as his moral qualities and disposition." The word *manaqib* is even associated with its own literary genre, the *manaqibnama*. Akın-Kıvanç points out that "with the emergence and spread of Sufism, *manaqibnama*s became a genre of hagiographical nature dealing exclusively with the lives and miraculous deeds of saintly figures."[56] The fact that Mustafa Ali uses the same word in the title of a work on artists is the strongest argument that, from our authors' perspective, artistic achievement cannot be properly understood without recourse to Sufi philosophy.

## 3. Ibn Arabi's Ontology

In a story entitled "Chinese Art and Greek Art," the renowned Sufi Jalaladdin Rumi (1207-1273).[1] forges a connection between Sufism and Ancient Greek philosophy.[2] The setting is a royal court where Chinese and Greek painters are engaged in a contest of skills. At first, the king orders a debate, but when the Chinese painters start to talk, the Greeks remain silent and leave. The Chinese painters then suggest that each party be given a room to demonstrate its skills, whereupon a large room is divided into two by a veil. While the Chinese request hundreds of colors from the king, the Greeks ask for no colors at all. As the Chinese start to paint, the Greeks simply clean and polish the walls on their side of the room. Once the Chinese have finished their painting, the king arrives in order to appraise both sides. The Greeks remove the veil dividing the room, and the Chinese painting reflects on their polished wall, showing itself even more stunningly than on the wall where it has been painted. "The Greek art," so Rumi, "is the Sufi way": it is not simply based on the mastery of knowledge and skill, but on the purification of heart and soul.[3]

Rumi's message is best understood via the writings of another prominent Sufi, Muhyiddin Ibn Arabi (1165-1240).[4] Ibn Arabi was a prolific writer,[5] but his ontology is succinctly expressed in his *Fusus al-Hikam* (The Bezels of Wisdom), composed in 1230. Described as the work in which Ibn Arabi "presents his thought in its maturest form,"[6] *The Bezels of Wisdom* outlines the philosopher's ontology in twenty-seven chapters, each named after a prophet in the Abrahamic-Islamic tradition and using that prophet as a starting point to illuminate a particular aspect of Ibn Arabi's thought.

Far from systematic in the philosophical sense, the work relies on a scattering of interrelated concepts that are repeated on hand of various examples throughout the text. This should not be misconstrued as randomness: the pedagogical goal of Ibn Arabi's style is to trigger unplanned mnemonic responses and elicit spontaneous flashes of insight from the reader. For the purposes of our present study, however, we will need to "reconstruct" Ibn Arabi's core concepts in a systematic fashion.

### The Veiling/Unveiling Cosmos

Ibn Arabi views the phenomenal world (the cosmos) as the self-disclosure of the hidden, divine mystery. Chapter 1 of *The Bezels of Wisdom* begins with the following statement:

> The Reality wanted to see the essences of His Most Beautiful Names or, to put it another way, to see His own Essence, in all-inclusive object encompassing the whole [divine] Command, which, qualified by existence, would reveal to Him His own mystery. For the seeing of a thing, itself by itself, is not the same as its seeing itself in another, as it were in a mirror; for it appears to itself in a form that is invested by the location of the vision by that which would only appear to it given the existence of the location and its [the location's] self-disclosure to it.[7]

The divine as transcendence, to Ibn Arabi, is beyond human cognition: he calls it "the Mystery of Mysteries"[8] or the "Absolute Mystery."[9] This is the divine aspect of stillness; it involves no self-manifestation (*tajalli*) of the divine. In fact, the divine cannot manifest itself in its absoluteness; transcending all relations and escaping all definition, it transcends even the concept of God (*Allah*), which only has meaning in relation to the concept of creation.[10] But since, as Toshihiko Izutsu puts it, "one cannot talk about anything at all without linguistic designation," Ibn Arabi "uses the word *haqq* (which literally means Truth or Reality) in referring to the Absolute."[11]

"Contemplation of the Reality without formal support is not possible," says Ibn Arabi, "since God, in His Essence, is far beyond all need of the Cosmos. [...] Therefore, some form of support is necessary."[12] In order to become knowable, then, the unknowable needs to manifest itself. This manifestation takes place through the phenomena, which serve to make the hidden mystery visible.[13] At the same time, though, the phenomena function as veils (*hijab*) that hide the mystery. As Ibn Arabi puts it,

> The Reality has described Himself as being hidden in veils of darkness, which are the natural forms, and by veils of light, which are the subtle spirits. The Cosmos consists of that which is gross and that which is subtle and is therefore, in both aspects, the veil [covering] its true self. For the Cosmos does not perceive the Reality as He perceives Himself, nor can it ever not be veiled.[14]

But while the particulars might function as veils, this does not mean they are mere obstacles to the perception of the reality. Rather, they are "veils" insofar as their very particularity makes it impossible for them to manifest the reality in its undifferentiated form. To describe the way in which the reality is perceived by the particulars *by way of* the particulars, Ibn Arabi turns to the metaphor of the mirror:

> A divine Self-revelation [...] occurs only in a form conforming to the essential predisposition of the recipient of such a revelation. Thus, the recipient sees nothing other than his own form in the mirror of the Reality. He does not see the Reality Itself, which is not possible, although he knows that he may see only his [true] form in It. As in the case of the mirror and the beholder, he sees the form in it, but does not see the mirror itself, despite his knowledge that he only sees his own and other images by means of it.[15]

The mirror, in making us visible to ourselves, becomes invisible itself. In order to *see* the image reflected, we need to *not see* the mirror itself. According to Ibn Arabi, a phenomenon is both a mirror and the image reflected onto it; an unveiling veil.

Ibn Arabi also explores the relationship between the manifest and the unmanifest through the concepts of dream (or imagination, *khayal*) and reality. The world of phenomena is a dream state, divorced from what he calls reality: "You are an imagination, as is all that you regard as other than yourself an imagination. All existence is an imagination within an imagination, the only Reality being God, as Self and the Essence."[16] As long as one revels in the world of particulars and severs ties with the hidden reality, the dream is a nightmare that repeats itself over and over again.

As we have seen, however, the phenomena serve to both veil *and* unveil. To Ibn Arabi, the dream state is full of symbols that point to the origin of the dream, i.e., reality. The phenomenal world must be interpreted, just like a dream, to reveal the truth it conceals: "When Muhammad said, 'All men are asleep and when they die they will awake,' he meant that everything a man sees in this life is of the same kind as that which one sleeping sees; in other words an apparition that requires interpretation."[17] "The interpreter," Ibn Arabi adds, "proceeds from the form seen by the dreamer to the form of the thing in itself, if he is successful."[18] In fact, such interpretation (*ta'wil*) is the only way to reach the hidden truth behind the phenomena.[19]

As an example of failed interpretation, Ibn Arabi offers the vision in which the prophet Abraham was urged by God to sacrifice his son. "Had he been true to the vision," Ibn Arabi states, "he would have killed his son, for he believed that it was his son he saw although with God it was nothing other than the Great Sacrifice in the form of his son." This, to the philosopher, was a failure on the prophet's part: "He did not interpret what he saw, but took it at its face value, although visions require interpretation."[20]

Ibn Arabi's view of the phenomenal world as a dream world does not imply a devaluation of the dream world as somehow "unreal" or "less real" than the reality.[21] The difference between the dream world and reality is that the former consists of individuals and particulars, subjects and objects, things that are distinct from each other, whereas in the latter, everything is united and one. However, we are not talking about two different worlds here, but rather two different perspectives on the same world: ultimately, to Ibn Arabi, dream and reality are only two aspects of the same unity. To awaken, then, means to comprehend the reality in its totality, from which perspective particularity and individuality appear like a dream.

In yet another way, the veiling function of phenomena is as important as their function of unveiling or manifestation, since the particulars could not bear experiencing the overwhelming reality of the hidden mystery in the absence of the phenomenal veil. The point is perfectly illustrated by the following *hadith*: "God hides Himself behind seventy thousand veils of light and darkness. If He took away these veils, the fulgurating lights of His face would at once destroy the sight of any creature who dared to look at it."[22]

We can conclude that the divine is engaged in a continuous movement of veiling (self-concealment) and unveiling (self-disclosure). As Ibn Arabi puts it,

> The Absolute [....] is nothing other than what comes out outwardly, whereas in the very moment of coming out outwardly it is what conceals itself inwardly. There is no one who sees the Absolute except the Absolute itself, and yet there is no one to whom the Absolute remains hidden. It is the Outward (i.e., self-manifesting) to itself, and yet it is the Inward (i.e., self-concealing) to itself.[23]

While the immanent, phenomenal world is the self-manifesting aspect of this strife and the transcendent absolute is its self-concealing aspect, the self-manifesting aspect also contains a strife within itself since it simultaneously unveils and veils the hidden.[24]

## The Human Being as Mirror

"The Reality," Ibn Arabi says, "gave existence to the whole Cosmos [at first] as an undifferentiated thing without anything of the spirit in it, so that it was like an unpolished mirror."[25] Spirit enters the cosmos by way of the human being: "Adam was the very principle of reflection for that mirror and the spirit of that form."[26] But the human being is both spirit and form, inner and outer alike: "his [man's] outer form He composed of the cosmic realities and forms, while his inner form He composed to match His Own form."[27] This commingling of the inner and outer makes the human being the "isthmus" (*barzakh*), the "essential link," so R.W.J. Austin, "between the Creator and His creation, that all-important medium by which God perceives Himself as manifested in the Cosmos, and by which the Cosmos recognizes its source in God."[28]

Ibn Arabi also describes the human being as the microcosm of the universe, or of the divine: "God has put into this noble epitome, the Perfect Man, all the Divine Names and the realities of all things existing outside of him in the Macrocosm which (apparently) subsist independently of him."[29] Just as the divine has two faces, namely the light (immanence) and the darkness (transcendence),[30] the human being also has two faces, one visible and one invisible. The visible body dwells in the realm of perception, while the invisible aspect, the soul or mind, belongs to the realm of reason. It is reason, or consciousness, that enshrines the human being's perfection as microcosm. In Izutsu's words,

> Man [...] not only synthesizes all the forms of the Divine self-manifestation which are scattered over the world of Being, but also is conscious of this whole. This is why a true comprehensive unity is established by Man, corresponding to the Unity of the Absolute. Man is in this sense the *Imago Dei*.[31]

Because it is the perfect microcosm, the human being can mirror the divine (the universe) as no other phenomenon can.

Ibn Arabi's division of the cosmos into visible and invisible is actually part of a more detailed scheme in which creation is divided into five planes (*hadarat*) of being that are based on Plato's analogy of the divided line. Ibn Arabi's planes are summarized by his disciple, al-Qashani,[32] as follows:

- The Plane of Senses and Sensible Experience, corresponding to Plato's "objects." This is the only purely material plane in the scheme.
- The Plane of Images and Imagination (*khayal*), roughly corresponding to Plato's "images." This plane is an intermediate realm between the sensible and spiritual worlds.
- The Plane of Actions or Spirits, roughly corresponding to Plato's "mathematical truths."
- The Plane of Attributes and Names, or of Intellects, roughly corresponding to Plato's "ideas" or "forms." The "Names" refer to Ibn Arabi's concept of "Permanent Archetypes," according to which all phenomenal existence is prefigured in archetypal form.
- The Plane of the Essence, of absolute non-manifestation, roughly corresponding to Plato's "Good." This is the only plane that stands outside manifestation.[33]

Plato and Ibn Arabi share the conviction that the lower planes are symbols of the higher ones,[34] and while the human being's body is related to the two lowest planes of existence, its invisible component is related to the remaining, higher planes.[35]

Still, Sufism does not advocate a renouncement of the body in favor of the mind/soul, but rather a unification of the two. This comes through in the favorable way Ibn Arabi compares humans to animals, who stand for the body without intellect,[36] and angels, who stand for the disembodied intellect.[37] Humans are superior to animals thanks to their minds and superior to the angels thanks to their bodies. When humans perceive, they do not perceive like a body without mind or a mind without body, but as a unity of body and mind. This unified view of body and mind also explains Sufism's philosophical emphasis on the phenomenal world as well as its practical emphasis on physical rituals such as music and dance.[38]

Such unity, however, cannot be taken for granted; it must first be achieved. If not, the body will remain a "particularizer" in the phenomenal world—as will the intellect, which creates dichotomies in its effort to know the unknowable, to understand the hidden reality. In Ibn Arabi's words, "The intellect restricts and seeks to define the truth within a particular qualification, while in fact the Reality does not admit of such a limitation."[39] Al-Qashani elaborates as follows:

> The "self-manifester," the locus of self-manifestation, the act of self-manifestation, the being of the self-manifester a self-manifester and the being of the locus a locus, etc. [....] are all notions conceived by our discriminating Reason, the distinctions existing only in our Reason. [....] There is nothing in Being except God![40]

The only way for a human being to catch a direct glimpse of reality is through the mystical experience of "self-annihilation" (*fana*), in which the dichotomy of body and mind is transcended. This experience is followed by the state of "subsistence" (*baqa*), in which one's self and appreciation of particulars are reinstated, but with the individual ego replaced by divine consciousness.[41] Only after such an experience and transformation do human beings achieve their full potential and deserve the title "Perfect Man" (*al-insan al-kamil*).[42]

Returning to the metaphor of the mirror, we could say that even though the divine discloses itself most fully via the human being, if the human being is not willing or able to reflect a perfect image of the divine, the disclosure cannot take place. The mirror of the human being must be polished to perfection before it can reflect the divine.[43]

The mystical experience of self-annihilation can be described as a metaphorical death, but Sufism maintains that a permanent unity between the soul and the divine, the perceiver and the perceived, or, one might say, the subject and the object, is only attainable in actual, physical death.[44] The allegorical story of Layla and Majnun, treated at greater length below, is a good example. Majnun, the symbol of the soul, is searching for his beloved Layla, the symbol of the Divine, in order to reunite with her. The unity is only achieved at the very end of the story, with the death of Majnun.[45]

This unity in death is described in one of Sufism's most famous metaphors, that of the ocean and the drop of water, which explores the relationship between the divine and the soul, or the absolute and the particulars. Being is considered to be like an ocean, while its particular manifestations resemble drops of water. The moment one particular comes into existence, it is like a drop of water splitting off from the ocean, and the moment it loses its particularity and dies, it merges again with the ocean from which it originates.[46] When you look at their "essence," a drop of water and the ocean are the same. One cannot claim that a drop of water carries less "truth" or "essence" than the ocean.[47]

## The Mystical Journey

Those who take the path of transcendence, to Ibn Arabi, are the prophet and the mystic, mirroring Plato's idea of the philosopher-king.[48] They undertake the "Gnostic ascent"[49] through the planes of being until the final mystical experience occurs in what al-Qashani describes as an "unveiling" (*kashf*).[50] This "unveiling" of reality is illustrated by Rumi through the metaphor of a wedding night. In traditional Islam, a man sees his bride, his beloved, for the first time on their wedding night. Similarly, the mystical experience takes place when the divine (the bride) is unveiled to the soul:

> The state is the unveiling of the bride,
> The station's being alone with her inside,
> For her unveiling's seen by every guest
> But with the groom alone the bride will rest—
> The bride unveils for every onlooker
> But afterwards he lies alone with her!
> So many Sufis have enjoyed a state
> But few know of the stations that await.[51]

To Ibn Arabi, the Gnostic ascent from the lower planes to the highest is the journey of the soul yearning for its beloved, the divine, from which it was separated by birth.[52]

Sufism holds that anyone with the right training can take this journey, attaining mystical knowledge of the primordial existence by "meeting the divine." Such knowledge goes beyond the descriptive capacity of human language, limited, as it is, by reason and the phenomenal world. Therefore, it reduces the mystic to a state of speechlessness. As Ibn Arabi puts it, "When

God established me in this station, I realized my animality to the full. I saw things and I wanted to express what I saw, but could not do so, being no different from those who cannot speak.".53 The prophet, however, completes the mystical circle and returns with a message, making the invisible visible to the rest of humankind..54 Prophets differ from regular mystics in that through their "messages," they teach us new ways of perception or thinking. They teach us how to see, that is, how to think..55

One Sufi story describes the mystical journey by way of a Sufi's physical journey from the East to the West, from home to the foreign, from the higher world in which the sun rises to the lower world in which it sets. The story, told in the *Canticle of the Birds* by Fariduddin Attar (ca. 1110-1221), introduces a well-respected sheikh, named San'an, who has many disciples..56 Whenever a disciple asks him to give an example of the divine, a glimpse of it at least, San'an says that the divine is "not this" or "not that." Instead of giving an affirmative description, he resorts to negations. One day, the sheikh dreams that he should take a journey to the West, to the Rome of the East, Constantinople. Following this command, he sets out on the road, accompanied by some of his disciples.

Upon arriving in Constantinople, he catches a glimpse of a Christian princess, immediately falling in love with her. His disciples are in shock on account of seeing their old, wise master in love with such a seemingly unsuitable object of desire. At first, the Christian princess rejects the love of the sheikh. After he stages many attempts to gain her affections, she decides to test his love and has him carry out a variety of tasks, such as drinking wine, herding swine, and even burning a copy of the Quran. Scandalizing his disciples, he performs all these demeaning tasks forbidden in Islam.

In the end, the Christian princess is so impressed by the sheikh that she converts to his religion. She ends up dying in his arms, and the sheikh finally returns home to the East. The story teaches us that unless the Sufi makes the journey from home to the foreign, thereby becoming homeless, it is impossible to perform the homecoming through which the mystical circle is completed.

Michael Barry interprets Sheikh San'an as a mystic who starts out by approaching the divine as unmanifest (transcendence) and later complements this understanding through an experience of the Divine as manifest (immanence):

> Attar's parable implies that his Arabian cleric—a walking caricature of the smug orthodox ordinary Muslim—remained far too content in his spiritual arrogance to worship only the invisible or Transcendental God in Mecca. This is why a divine voice urged this very cleric to travel humbly to Christian Byzantium, in order to learn there the secret of the Immanent God made visible through Creation's lovely forms or manifest "icons." [....] Attar's cleric finally attains complete wisdom by perceiving God as both Transcendent and as Immanent, and the Greek princess falls at his feet in turn..[57]

Also contained in the tale is Sufism's take on the three Abrahamic religions. At first, the sheikh only knows one aspect of the divine: the hidden, the dark, the absolute Other, a God who can only be described *via negativa*, exemplified by the Judaic God in the writings of Moses Maimonides..[58] Christianity differentiates itself from this approach with its strong emphasis on God as manifested, exemplified by Christ as divinity incarnate..[59] This emphasis also accounts for the significant role that paintings of the divine have played in Christianity (and, specifically, Christian churches) in contrast to the other Abrahamic religions. Via his journey, the sheikh learns from Christianity that the divine is not only darkness but also light, manifesting itself through creation.[60]

Sufism, I would argue, aims at a synthesis of the Judaic and Christian approaches. Muhammad, described by Sufis as the "Seal of the Prophets,"[61] combines the two worldviews of the divine as manifest and unmanifest, thereby "sealing" the philosophical route opened up by the Abrahamic tradition. As Izutsu puts it, "According to Ibn 'Arabi, the ideal combination of *tanzih* [transcendence] and *tashbih* [immanence] was achieved only in Islam."[62]

## Beyond Dichotomies

The highest aim of Ibn Arabi's ontology is to attain the ultimate truth, which is the unity of the divine and the soul, darkness and light, or, one might say, noumena and phenomena. The concept of unity helps Ibn Arabi overcome a dichotomy between the Judaic and Christian traditions, takes him beyond Platonic dualism into the realm of Neoplatonism, and, as we will see further below, renders his thought incompatible with the dualistic Cartesian worldview.

Throughout *The Bezels of Wisdom*, Ibn Arabi explicitly recoils from the temptation of dualism in whatever guise it may appear—and the guises are many. About the dichotomy between creator and created, he has the following to say:

> When you consider His saying, "I am his foot with which he walks, his hand with which he strikes, and his tongue with which he speaks," and all the other faculties and members in which they are situated, why do you make the distinction by saying it is all the Reality, or it is all created? It is all created in a certain sense, but it is also the Reality in another sense.[63]

The dichotomy between transcendence and immanence is equally rejected:

> The intellect, by itself, absorbing knowledge in its own way, knows only according to the transcendental and nothing of the immanental. It is only when God acquaints it with His Self-manifestation that its knowledge of God becomes complete, seeing Him as transcendent when appropriate, and as immanent when appropriate..[64]

Ibn Arabi also has no patience for the dichotomy between the observer and the observed:

> Positing something other than what is looked on, thus establishing a relation between two things, the observer and the thing observed, nulli[fies] the Unity, although [in reality] only He sees Himself alone through Himself. Here also there would appear to be observer and observed [but both are He]..[65]

Along with the idea of duality, that of multiplicity is abandoned as well:

> The perfect gnostic is one who regards every object of worship as a manifestation of God in which He is worshiped. They call it a god, although its proper name might be stone, wood, animal, man, star, or angel. Although that might be its particular name, Divinity presents a level that causes the worshiper to imagine that it is his object of worship. In reality, this level is the Self-manifestation of God to the consciousness of the worshiper in this particular mode of manifestation..[66]

One of the most challenging dichotomies tackled by Ibn Arabi is that between male and female. At first glance, it would appear that a clear hierarchy is involved: woman is created from man just as the cosmos is created from the absolute, with activity assigned to the male and passivity to the female.[67] In Ibn Arabi's words:

> God drew forth from him a being in his own image, called woman, and because she appears in his own image, the man feels a deep longing for her, as something yearns for itself, while she feels longing for him as one who longs for that place to which one belongs.[68]

Ultimately, however, Ibn Arabi turns this dichotomy on its head as well, giving us an image of the feminine divine by describing the creation of the cosmos as an act of giving birth. Creation, to the philosopher, may be likened to a divine exhalation, described as the "Breath of the Merciful" (*nafas al-rahman*), whereby the word for "mercy" (*rahmah*) derives from that for "womb" (*rahim*).[69]

In the final chapter of *The Bezels of Wisdom*, Ibn Arabi goes to some length in emphasizing the feminine nature of the divine creative act. Starting from a *hadith* that quotes the prophet Muhammad as saying, "Of all the things of your world, three things have been made particularly dear to me, women, perfumes, and the ritual prayer,"[70] the philosopher stages a linguistic analysis, maintaining that the words for "woman" and "prayer" are feminine in Arabic, and that the common plural for the set of three, which should be masculine according to Arabic grammar, was also rendered feminine by the prophet.[71] Proceeding from this linguistic assessment to an ontological assertion, Ibn Arabi goes on to state that:

> The man finds himself situated between an essence [i.e., the Divine Essence] which is his [ontological] source and a woman [i.e., his own mother] who is his [physical] source. Thus he is placed between two feminine nouns, that is to say, between the femininity of essence and the real [i.e., physical] femininity.[72]

Women, to Ibn Arabi, are the perfect manifestation of the feminine creative principle of the divine. When a man contemplates the beauty of a woman, the philosopher states, "It is none other than He whom he sees in her.".[73] "The Apostle [Muhammad]," he goes on, "loved woman by reason of perfect contemplation of the Reality in them.".[74] Ultimately, the divine is both male and female, and both male and female are active and passive alike.

Ibn Arabi resolves all dichotomies, such as those listed above, in a *coincidentia oppositorum*.[75] that is only accessible through the experience of "unveiling" but that, on the level of rational thought and language, only leaves the speaker with a set of contradictory and paradoxical statements:

> You may say of Being what you will; either that it is the creation or that it is the Reality, or that it is at once the creation and the Reality. It might also be said that there is neither creation nor the Reality, as one might admit to perplexity in the matter, since by assigning degrees the difficulties appear..[76]

The oneness of being (*wahdah al-wujud*) is often explained by Sufis with reference to the Muslim confession of faith, "No God, But God" (*la ilaha illa-llah*). In Sufism, "No God" refers to the darkness or hidden divine, while "But God" refers to the light or unconcealed divine. The divine is neither just the unconcealed nor just the concealed—it is both at the same time, and Ibn Arabi does not grant superiority to either aspect:

> The transcendent Reality is the relative creature, even though the creature be distinct from the Creator. The Reality is at once the created Creator and the creating creature. All this is One Essence, at once Unique and Many..[77]

To Ibn Arabi, the "image," the reflection in the mirror, is not merely a reflection of a thing in itself, but the unmanifest in manifested form—it is the visibility of the invisible. Ultimately, Sufism rejects the distinction between the thing in itself (the essence) and the phenomena. Phenomena already carry the very same odor (essence) as noumena.

A Sufi metaphor illustrating this point is that of the candle and the mirror. Picture a candle holder with a mirror attached to augment the light of the candle. The candle, here, stands for the divine, and the mirror for the manifestation (specifically, the human soul).[78] Qualitatively, there is no difference between the light produced by the candle and that emanating from the mirror. As Rumi's Greek painters were well aware, a perfect reflection and the object reflected are the same.

## Interdependence of Reality and Cosmos

Proceeding from the oneness of being, Ibn Arabi rejects any hierarchy in the relationship between the reality and the cosmos, the transcendent and the immanent, or the concealed and the unconcealed. Rather, he sees the relationship as one of interdependence. The creator needs the creation, and human beings in particular, since divine self-knowledge remains incomplete without knowledge of the divine as manifested. In Ibn Arabi's words, "The image of perfection is complete only with knowledge of both the ephemeral and the eternal, the rank of knowledge being perfected only by both aspects."[79]

Regarding human beings in particular, Ibn Arabi maintains that "It is we who make Him a divinity by being that through which He knows Himself as Divine. Thus, He is not known until we are known."[80] Human consciousness acts as the intermediary through which the divine perceives the cosmos: "For the Reality, he is as the pupil is for the eye through which the act of seeing takes place. Thus he is called *insan* [meaning both man and pupil], for it is by him that the Reality looks on His creation.".[81] Hence, the creator and human beings act as mirrors and even as nourishment for each other: "You are His nourishment as bestowing the contents of His Self-Knowledge, while He is yours as bestowing existence, which is assigned to you being assigned also to Him.".[82] The issue is perfectly summarized by Ibn Arabi in the following poem:

He praises me and I praise Him,
He worships me and I worship Him.
[…]
Where then is His Self-sufficiency,
Since I help Him and grant Him Bliss?
It is for this that the Reality created me,
For I give content to His Knowledge and manifest Him..[83]

Ibn Arabi maintains that the very concept of a god or lord is meaningless without the complementary concept of a servant, rendering the former dependent on the latter. "Divinity," he says, "implies and requires that which depends on it, just as Lordship requires servanthood, since neither would have any existence or meaning otherwise.".[84] The servants, through their actions, condition the reactions of the lord as much as vice versa: "The whole Cosmos subjects, by circumstance, One Who cannot properly be called subjected, as He has said, 'Every day He is busy with some matter.'".[85] This subjection of the lord by the servant, or the creator by the creation, is likened by Ibn Arabi to the responsibilities that conscientious rulers assume vis-à-vis their subjects: "Some kings strive for their own ends, while others realize the truth of the matter and know that by rank they are in subjection to their own subjects.".[86]

The interdependence of essence and existence is also expressed in Ibn Arabi's concept of "bipolar triplicity".[87] As R.W.J. Austin puts it, creation occurs in a triplicity consisting of "Essential Oneness, the urge to polarity, and the actual experience of bipolarity, which itself is eternally being resolved back into the Essence".[88] This triplicity is bipolar in that it cannot simply exist on the part of the creator but must be mirrored in the creation as well. According to Ibn Arabi, the creation participates in the bipolar triplicity as follows: "Its latent essence in its state of nonexistence corresponds to the Essence of its Creator, its 'hearing' [receptivity] to the Will of its Creator, and its compliance with the Creative Command to His saying [Word] *Be*".[89] Rather than being a passive outcome, the created is actively involved in its own creation: "In truth, it was none other than the thing itself that brought itself into being from nonexistence when the Command was given".[90]

Finally, Ibn Arabi views the process of creation as perpetual, recurring, and fundamentally unstable.[91] "Every Self-manifestation," he maintains, "at once provides a creation and annihilates another. Its annihilation is extinction at the [new] Self-manifestation, subsistence being what is given by the following Self-manifestation".[92] This perpetual process of creation and annihilation is tied to the "Breath of the Merciful": "God is manifest in every Breath and [...] no Self-manifestation is repeated".[93] Ibn Arabi even rejects the idea that the creator comes first in time: "Although He is the First, no temporal priority may be attributed of Him. Thus He is called also the Last. [....] He is called the Last only in the sense that all reality, though reality be attributed to us, is His".[94]

If the light (the unconcealed) and the darkness (the concealed) are neither dichotomous and separate nor one and the same, how are we to understand the relationship between them?

I propose the following approach: In talking about the inscrutable darkness of the divine, Ibn Arabi can be taken to view the divine as potentiality, an infinite potentiality that can give birth to infinite numbers of self-manifestations or particulars. If so, what grounds these manifestations is not some kind of independently existing, ultimate reality, but rather the potentiality of creation. Therefore, I would argue, Sufism allows for the interpretation that there is no existence beyond existence. Beyond actuality, there is only potentiality.

## 4. Sufism and Miniature Painting

Equipped with this outline of Ibn Arabi's ontology, let us now return to our sources on miniature painting and see how they forge the connection between Sufi philosophy and art. One of our authors, Mustafa Ali, even works a direct reference to Ibn Arabi into his text. To be sure, this is not a citation in the modern sense, but rather a mention of Ibn Arabi's year of death, indicating Mustafa Ali's knowledge of, and reverence for, the "great shaykh."[1]

### Ibn Arabi in Dust Mohammad

Apart from this direct reference, the most obvious sign of a shared Sufi ontology underlying the works of our authors and Ibn Arabi can be found in Dust Mohammad, who starts his treatise as follows:

> The coalesced forms and dispersed shapes of the archetypes were hidden in the recesses of the unseen in accordance with the dictum, "I was a hidden treasure."
>
> Then, in accordance with the words, "I wanted to be known, so I created creation in order to be known," he snatched with the fingers of destiny the veil of non-existence from the countenance of being, and with the hand of mercy and the pen, which was "the first thing God created," he painted masterfully on the canvas of being.[2]

This passage is basically a reformulation of the opening lines to Chapter 1 of *The Bezels of Wisdom*, as we read above:

> The Reality wanted to see the essences of His Most Beautiful Names or, to put it another way, to see His own Essence, in all-inclusive object encompassing the whole [divine] Command, which, qualified by existence, would reveal to Him His own mystery.[3]

Dust Mohammad takes up the Sufi ideas of divine transcendence, the prefiguration of phenomenal existence in archetypal form, and the self-manifestation of the divine through the phenomena, all elaborated by Ibn Arabi.[4] He then combines these ideas with a metaphor of God as painter, whose self-manifestation is compared to an act of artistic—and specifically painterly—expression. This metaphor forges a bridge between Sufi thought and miniature art that will be crossed repeatedly both in the remainder of Dust Mohammad's text and by our other authors.

The Ibn Arabi passage continues with the words, "For the seeing of a thing, itself by itself, is not the same as its seeing itself in another, as it were in a mirror."[5] Here, the philosopher introduces his central metaphor of the mirror, which Dust Mohammad also takes up in his treatise, describing how God:

> cleansed from the tablet of his being the dust of nonexistence with the polish of favor; and in the heights indicated the words, "Assume the characteristics of God," he made the mirror of creation a locus of manifestation for names and traces.[6]

Towards the end of his Preface, Dust Mohammad returns to the mirror with a short passage in verse:

> When the desired form is manifested from the
> invisible world, like a mirror, the surface of a
> pure heart is best.[7]

Dust Mohammad is also familiar with Ibn Arabi's metaphor of phenomena as veils that both conceal and reveal the divine: we see this both in his above reference to God lifting "the veil of nonexistence from the countenance of being" and in a later reference to the miniaturist Ahmad Musa, who "lifted the veil from the face of depiction."[8]

Further, Dust Mohammad shares Ibn Arabi's conception of the prophet Muhammad not just as the messenger of God, but also the "Seal of the Prophets" and the archetypal "perfect man" who pre-exists the creation of the universe and embodies the human perfection for which the followers of the Sufi path strive. Ibn Arabi cites a *hadith* according to which Muhammad "was a prophet when Adam was still between the water and the clay," and adds that the prophet "is the most perfect creation of this humankind, for which reason the whole affair [of creation] begins and ends with him.".[9] These ideas are echoed in Dust Mohammad, who describes the prophet as "That perfect human, the outline of whose noble-fruited tree was the first form to appear from the pure light of existence on the page of being".[10] and adds that the prophet was the "Seal whose ring of power is decorated with the legend, 'I was a prophet while Adam was between water and clay.'".[11]

A lengthy story that Dust Mohammad relates about the art of painting forcefully illustrates the link between his and Ibn Arabi's thought. As we saw above, Dust Mohammad holds that "by the externality of the religious law, the masters of depiction hang their heads in shame,".[12] but nonetheless maintains that "portraiture is not without justification, and the portraitist's conscience need not be pricked by the thorn of despair.".[13] This "justification," the author informs us, derives from the fact that the art of painting "originated with the prophet Daniel.".[14]

How does this prophetic origin come about? According to Dust Mohammad, "after the prophet's [Muhammad's] death, some of his companions went to Byzantium with the purpose of presenting Islam. In that realm they met an emperor named Hercule.".[15] The emperor shows the prophet's companions a chest that contains a series of wondrous portraits. Presenting the first portrait, the emperor proclaims:

"This [...] is a portrait of Adam, the Father of Humanity." And thus he continued to show portraits until he produced one with a miraculous visage as luminous as the sun, whose regal being took Adam from the dust of nonexistence and garbed him with the cloak of purity. The admiration that the former portrait had elicited from the onlookers was nullified by the sight of this blessed face, and the perplexity with which they had been struck by the first portrait's beauty ceased with the contemplation of the sun-like beauty of the latter.[16]

This final portrait, of course, is that of the prophet Muhammad. The emperor goes on to explain that the portraits, far from having been painted to represent the physical appearances of the prophets, were created prior to the prophets' phenomenal existence and reflect them in their archetypal, uncreated aspect:

"Adam besought the Divine Court to see the prophets among his offspring," said Hercule. "Therefore the Creator of All Things sent a chest containing several thousand compartments, in each of which was a piece of silk on which was a portrait of one of the prophets. Inasmuch as that chest came as a witness, it was called the Chest of Testimony. After attaining his desire Adam placed the chest in his treasure house, which was near the setting place of the sun. Dhu'l-Qarnayn [Alexander the Great] carried it away and gave it to the prophet Daniel, who copied [the portraits] with his miraculous brush."[17]

Concerned as it is with the prophets' ontological qualities rather than their physical appearances and worldly deeds,[18] the portrait chest of Byzantium seems like a pictorial version of *The Bezels of Wisdom*. Ibn Arabi's masterpiece performs the exact same exercise in written form, taking its reader beyond the worldly existence of the prophets on a quest for the ontological meaning underlying these manifestations. In light of all the above, it would be no exaggeration to describe Dust Mohammad as an author whose ontological framework was wholly determined by Sufism in general and Ibn Arabi in particular.

### Creator as Artist, Artist as Creator

As we have seen, Dust Mohammad describes the deity as a painter who uses "being" as a canvas for his self-expression. Elevating the arts by linking them to divine creative activity is a metaphorical approach employed by all our authors. Qadi Ahmad initially presents the deity as a scribe:

> The pre-eternal scribe of the folio of Thy royalty
> Has written it with the pen of Predestination upon the Tablet of Fate.[19]

"The first object created by the Creator was the *qalam* [pen] of marvelous writing,"[20] Qadi Ahmad writes, echoing the Quran, which posits this archetypal pen as the deity's first creation.[21] "Through the *qalam*," he explains, "existence receives God's orders."[22] Mustafa Ali joins Qadi Ahmad in his praise of the pen as a divine creative instrument:

> O Pen! Never has your wisdom executed on the pages of the universe
> A faulty sketch or a faulty line.[23]

While Mustafa Ali never describes the deity as a painter, Dust Mohammad—always—and Qadi Ahmad—at certain points—take this path. The latter has the deity adorning "the pages of changing time with the motley black-and-white design of nights becoming days and days becoming nights,"[24] and arranging "the album of the revolving skies with the multicolored pages of spring and autumn."[25] And the former devotes some quite flowery passages to divine creation as painting:

Sometimes he makes black pens from the eyelashes of the *houris* and draws the tresses of beauties on the face of day from the inkpot of night, and sometimes he makes a pen of sunrays and moonbeams and draws the shapes of beauties with the blood of lovers on the canvas of loveliness.[26]

In the following poem, Dust Mohammad's deity is a painter of human faces and shapes:

He clothed each one in a color, a color of God's tincture, without hesitation.

He adorned one beautifully with mole and down: a whole worldful fell into error on account of its beauty.

To another he gave a seditious eye that would shed blood with blood-dripping dagger [eyelashes].

Around the lips of another he drew a novel design, by means of which animating down souls were pawned.

For yet another he innovated a fascinating stature, casting calamity into the heart from the world above....

If a form is not worthy of astonishment, it is not worth a touch of the brush.

[...]

The eternal painter who drew that black line, O Lord, what marvelous shapes are in his pen![27]

Dust Mohammad also renders the deity as both writer and painter. And since both activities mirror divine creativity, the author presents them as forms of worship:

The noblest rescript with which the scribes of the workshop of prayer adorn the album of composition and novelty, and the most subtle picture with which the depictors of the gallery of intrinsic meaning decorate the assemblies of creativity and invention, is praise of the Creator, by whose pen are scriven sublime letters and exalted forms.[28]

While divine creation and artistic production might be metaphorically linked, they are by no means the same. "Where the perfect swiftness of creation and destiny is," Dust Mohammad asks, "what room is there for the depiction of the pen or the pen of depiction?"[29] In another poem, the author concedes that his description of the deity as painter is merely a metaphor that fails to grasp the overwhelming awesomeness of divine creation:

> Neither is his destining in need of machination nor is his depiction dependent upon the pen.
> He quickened thousands of charming forms: neither did he use a magic incantation nor did he mix colors.[30]

Such disclaimers notwithstanding, the comparison of deity and artist lets a genie out of the bottle that our authors are never quite able to contain again. What if art as a human endeavor produces more than a mere representation of the perceptible world? What if art unconceals being in a way not possible without art's intervention?

The question arises even for calligraphy, an art form usually viewed as religiously unassailable. As Barry informs us, "Eastern Islamic mystical speculation in the fifteenth and sixteenth centuries [...] came to invest the calligraphic stroke [...] with 'the breath of life': that is, the 'divine breath' or 'holy spirit' of creation, called in Arabic the *ruh*."[31] With calligraphy, however, it is never quite clear whether the divine inspiration comes from the art itself or from the meaning of the words that the art is used to convey. After all, our authors describe the deity as a scribe rather than a calligrapher, implying that it is the content of the message, rather than the form of its delivery, that renders the art of writing divinely sanctioned. It is not so much calligraphy that creates; rather, the creative impetus belongs to the words that are expressed through calligraphy.

Our authors reinforce this argument in many ways. Qadi Ahmad quotes Maulana Sultan Ali: "Writing exists in order to be read. Not that (readers) should get stuck in it."[32] And Mustafa Ali connects "the nobility of calligraphy" to "the necessity of writing."[33] For both authors, calligraphy is inextricably entangled with the meaning of the words it conveys—the words, of course, being the verses of the Quran. Calligraphy is literal: it cannot transcend words to communicate something beyond them, something words themselves do not already contain and express in an explicit or implicit fashion. This tethering of calligraphy to specific words and meanings renders the art religiously safe—but also severely limits its aspirations.

While calligraphy is limited by the written word, the written word itself has fatal limitations in Sufi philosophy. As Annemarie Schimmel puts it, "letters might be a veil between [Sufis] themselves and the immediate experience of the Divine, for which the mind and the heart have to be like a blank page."[34] The written word is equated here with the "letter of the law," or an unreflective observation of the ritualistic side of religion, while Sufis pursued the "spirit of the law" through unmediated experience.

The illiteracy of the prophet Muhammad is used by all three of our authors to drive home this exact point. To Dust Mohammad, the prophet is "The unlettered one who has drawn, without aid of the pen, a line of abrogation through a thousand books."[35] Mustafa Ali writes that "his rising above the passion for the black [ink] of reading and writing [indicated] that perpetual sciences and eternal knowledge were inscribed in the black core of his heart."[36] And Qadi Ahmad uses the following passage from Maulana Sultan Ali to approach the issue:

As Mustafa [Muhammad] enjoyed the grace of the Lord
He had no need to read and write.
To him from Pre-eternity became known
All that had been traced by the Pen of Creation.[37]

What all these passages share is the Sufi understanding of the written word as a mediator and, therefore, strictly speaking, a veil or an obstacle between the human being and her apprehension of the absolute. Immediate perception or experience, as in the case of the prophet, is always to be preferred to the mediated perception enabled by the written word. In light of this, it is little wonder that many Sufis regarded the illiterate Muhammad, in Ladan Akbarnia and Francesca Leoni's words, as "the model for all Sufis and 'the first link in the spiritual chain of Sufism.'"[38]

The insufficiency of words—whether written or, indeed, spoken—takes us back, once again, to Ibn Arabi and Rumi. Ibn Arabi, as we know, regarded direct experience of the absolute as absolutely incommunicable: "I saw things and I wanted to express what I saw, but could not do so, being no different from those who cannot speak."[39] Rumi expresses the same idea in poetic form:

While explanation sometimes makes things clear
True love through silence only one can hear:
The pen would smoothly write the things it knew
But when it came to love it split in two.[40]

If I describe this it will be in vain;
What lies beyond words how can I explain?
This mystery would smash your brain to bits;
When writing it the firmest stylus splits.[41]

Here, then, we have identified the fatal flaw of calligraphy from the viewpoint of Sufi philosophy, if calligraphy is understood as a tool for apprehending the divine. This flaw bedevils the art not in spite of, but because of its symbiotic relationship with the letter of Islamic revelation. It was not just that calligraphy could not go beyond the written word; the written word itself could not go beyond descriptive or conceptual thought; and such thought was unable to either grasp or communicate absolute reality. To Sufi philosophy, then, calligraphy had to remain but a representation of a representation of the unrepresentable absolute.

## *Miniature Art and the Self-Manifestation of the Absolute*

This is where the temptation of miniature art becomes apparent. Our authors display an awed if conflicted awareness that painting is able to manifest something that goes beyond words. "According to these authors," Akın-Kıvanç writes, "most of whom were practicing calligraphers, the wondrous elements of the art of painting were not explicable by words. In his Preface, for example, Dust Mohammad writes that Bihzad's painting is 'beyond all description.'"[42] Not only is painting inexplicable, it is also capable of "innovation"—of producing something new, unseen, and unheard of.[43] Above, we saw Dust Mohammad use words like "innovate" and "astonishment" when describing the deity's (metaphorical) painterly work. Similarly, Mustafa Ali describes the miniaturist Muhammad of Herat as "the master of confounding innovations."[44]

What are we to make of this relatively vague nomenclature? What do the authors have in mind when they talk of innovation, inexplicability, and astonishment? Are they simply employing literary clichés—somewhat like "a beauty beyond words"—or is there a further depth of thought to be plumbed beneath these assertions?

To answer these questions, I will turn to two historical figures that have been mythologized in the miniature tradition:

the painter Kamaluddin Bihzad of Herat (ca. 1465-1533) and Mani, the prophet of the Manichaean religion (ca. 216-273). Often named in the same breath, these two are the pinnacles of artistic excellence to our authors: "By his sketches and his paintings he called to mind the image of Mani and the master Behzad Harawi," Qadi Ahmad writes about Ibrahim Mirza,[45] while Mustafa Ali honors a certain Master Qudrat as "a master of Mani-like qualities and Bihzad-like artistry."[46]

The most legendary painter of the miniature tradition,[47] Bihzad passed his early career at the court of Husayn Bayqara, the last Timurid ruler of Herat and an exceptional patron of the arts.[48] At the beginning of the 16th century, the city experienced a period of extreme instability in which it was conquered first by the Uzbeks (1507) and subsequently by Ismail I, founder of the Safavid dynasty (1510). Briefly falling to the Uzbeks again after Ismail's death, the city was retaken by the Safavid ruler Tahmasp in 1528.

Due to the city's precarious fortunes, its artistic milieus started dispersing, and Bihzad entered the patronage of the Safavids. He became a favorite of Ismail I, who proclaimed him, in 1522, "as overseer of all library workshops in the Safavid Empire—in effect, as the recognized master of all artists of the book."[49] Under Ismail's successor Tahmasp, Bihzad maintained his stature until his death in 1533, when he was buried, so Dust Mohammad, "next to the grave of the great poet Shaykh Kamal in Tabriz."[50]

Bihzad's relationship to Ismail was of such proximity as to inspire legends. In *Epic Deeds of Artists*, Mustafa Ali recounts one such legend from an Ottoman perspective, i.e., the perspective of the Safavids' enemies. Ismail's forces are about to clash with those of his nemesis, the Ottoman Sultan Selim I, on the Chaldiran Plain in 1514.

Shah Ismail first hid the praiseworthy [calligrapher] Shah Mahmud Nijad and then the matchless figural-painter Master Bihzad in a cavern, saying, "Who knows, should flight or death befall my body, and destruction and chaos the land of Persia, they might fall prey to the God-empowered hand of Sultan Salim Khan of Rum."[51][....] [Then, following the battle, Ismail] first went to the place where he had lodged them and searched for them. When he found [the two] where he had left [them], he was filled with gratitude to the Lord of Power from the depths of his heart.[52]

Bihzad is the "archetype of artistic excellence"[53] against whom our authors measure all other miniature painters. But what made his paintings so special? In the following couplet, Qadi Ahmad offers a clue:

His images of birds are heart ravishing,
Like the birds of Christ they acquire a soul.[54]

Bihzad's paintings, then, are described as bestowing souls upon their subjects. A further examination by Qadi Ahmad reveals this very life-giving quality as the core of what makes painting innovative, astonishing, and inexplicable.

Well-done, the magic-working masters of the brush
Whose bewitching tool bestows a new life.
They come to grips with every creature
And conjure up to life the likeness of everyone;
In creating they are followers of the pure godhead,
From the encompassing circle of the sky to the surface of the earth.
They cast their glances about creation
And make copies of every original.
Their creative art is a guide to the plan of the universe,
With them the *qalam* is bent in prostration (before God).
I cannot understand with what art they treat images
So that they seem to be speaking to men.[55]

Innovation, here, seems to consist of "bestowing new life" where there was none before. The process by which miniaturists produce this "life" is that which "cannot be understood." And astonishment is what results when such a painting, seemingly "speaking to men," is witnessed by a beholder. Nonetheless, Qadi Ahmad clearly speaks of miniaturists as "making copies" of "originals." They are not originators, but "followers" of divine creation. Are we, then, to conclude that bestowing "life" simply consisted of an extremely developed realism, endowing certain paintings with a high degree of verisimilitude?

To answer this question, we must now turn to the figure of Mani. The historical Mani, prophet of Manichaeism, was born in Babylonia around the year 216. He was mainly active under the Sassanian ruler Shapur I (r. 241-272) and was executed around 273, briefly after Shapur's death.[56] Mani, who truly appears to have painted,[57] is transformed by the miniature tradition into a kind of anti-Bihzad, an artist who abused his astounding talent to pretend he could create life, and who used this pretense to back up his false claim to prophethood. Dust Mohammad sums the story up as follows:

> Mani began to pretend to prophesy and made this claim acceptable in the eyes of the people by cloaking it in portraiture. Since the people expected a miracle of him, he took a span of silk, went into a cave and ordered the entrance closed. When one year had passed from the time of his withdrawal, he emerged and showed the silk. On it he had painted and portrayed the likenesses of humans, animals, trees, birds and various shapes that occur only in the mirror of the mind through the eye of imagination and that sit on the page of possibility in the visible world only with fantastic shapes.[58]

The author dismisses Mani's "pretense" to prophecy, stating that "The short-sighted ones whose turbid hearts could not reflect the light of Islam [were] duped by his game."[59] Still, it is clear that Mani had extraordinary skill in depicting both fantastic beings and ones that actually existed. The following story by Mustafa Ali confirms Mani's skill. It all begins with three court painters who devise a challenge to outperform and humiliate any painter who dares to take it up.

> They went out to a royal garden on the outskirts of the city. [There,] they painted [an] image of an abundant stream and a fountain that gushed sweet waters. Playing a trick, they sent forth those who claimed to be artists to the non-existent stream by that fountainhead [from whence they] brought back no water. As a result of that ploy, each of the masters who arrived at that fountain broke his jug while attempting to collect its water, and out of embarrassment, instead of returning to the masters, they chose to flee [that] land.[60]

Clearly, what is at issue here is verisimilitude or realism, with the three masters producing a *trompe-l'œil* that no other artist can distinguish from the actual garden surrounding it. Finally, Mani, a young artist "who did not have much of a reputation,"[61] decides to take up the challenge.

> At the place of trial, [upon seeing] the pieces of jars left by those whose offering cups had been broken and whose dignity and honor had been humiliated, the sweet waters of his nature became disturbed.
> [....]
> Instantly, he grabbed his wonder-working reed pen [...]. That fine-sketching pen, rendering a dog's carcass with assurance, brought forth an esoteric creation and made manifest a flawless magic painting. So much so that the worms on the corpse were visible, and furthermore, they all [were] moving and quivering. In every respect, it [was] unmistakably a beast's carcass. It was evident that, but for the missing smell, it had no defect. And, it [was] clear as day that each one of the

moving and writhing worms completely made up for that shortcoming."[62]

Mani returns to the three masters with his empty jug, telling them he could not retrieve the water since a dog's carcass had poisoned the fountain's contents. Upon inspecting the modified painting, the masters are forced to concede Mani's superior skill.

It may seem that Mani prevails through his ability to match—or perhaps even exceed—the masters' realism. However, the issue is not that simple. Mani's victory here is of a moral as much as an artistic nature. His motivation is not just the desire to outperform the masters, but also the outrage he feels on behalf of the previous competitors "whose dignity and honor had been humiliated." And his artistic response is of a similarly moral kind: the worms eating the rotting dog's carcass symbolize the hubris eating away at the three masters' personalities. In his moral response, then, Mani stands firmly in the tradition of holistic perfection outlined above, according to which an artist's skills could only be a reflection of his moral qualities.

Mustafa Ali is quite unique in this positive spin on the controversial figure of Mani—a spin that may well have scandalized Dust Mohammad. But he also goes further than Dust Mohammad in assessing the artistic accomplishments of Mani. The following passage finds Mani not copying existing things or conjuring up fantastic shapes, but rather granting visibility to phenomena that patently exist but are normally invisible.

Certain things, such as a blowing wind or a boisterous, rushing storm, that were impossible to represent as matter and give a visible form, [he would render] in different ways so their depiction would be veiled. The said master Mani possessed such artistry and creativity that when he depicted flowing water, he would make it visible in crystal-like form, and when he depicted a blowing wind, he would make it manifest like an abundant stream.[63]

Paradoxically, the painter manages to depict water in "crystal-like form" while enabling the eye to witness its "flow." Similarly, he manages to paint a visible wind by endowing it with the attributes of a stream. He "veils" the depiction of these phenomena, meaning, with Ibn Arabi, that he unconceals them in the very act of concealing them.

This take on Mani's art as a unique form of unconcealment is also found in Mustafa Ali's next anecdote. Here, the artist has joined the three masters in the service of their lord. As in Rumi's story about Chinese and Greek painters, each artist is ordered by the sovereign—the "ruler of China"—to decorate one wall of a hall. Just as in Rumi, the artists work "behind a veil," with their art invisible to the others. And once again, Mustafa Ali singles out Mani's work for particular praise:

> He showed that, with various tricks and variegated colors, it was possible to embellish the beauties that the Artist of Imagination did not impart on the Tablet of mind and the arts that the Painter of Perfection did not render on the slate of intellect.[64]
>
> [....]
>
> In other words, that peerless master gave the wall such a burnishing that pure water has never been so transparent. And he gave his every image such a bright appearance that the world-illuminating mirror has never furbished plants and flowers in that tone.
>
> [....]
>
> With their pure, natural quality, Mani's
> Designs became a mirror for his enemies.
>
> > He gave [his] world[-renowned] pictures such a light that
> > From end to end they began to manifest God's providence.[65]

Once again, we are forced to distinguish the Mani we find in Mustafa Ali from the one in Dust Mohammad. Mustafa Ali's Mani is morally impeccable, and rather than "dupe" people, his art "manifests God's providence" in an authentic fashion. It is also notable that nowhere in Mustafa Ali's account do we find mention of Mani's "false" claim to prophecy. But our main interest here lies not in contrasting depictions of Mani in Islamic sources, but in what these depictions can tell us about the Sufi understanding of art. And viewed from that perspective, the above passages are nothing short of remarkable.

Mustafa Ali posits here that art can constitute a manifestation of the divine absolute that is not only different from other phenomena, but actually enables these phenomena to reach a state of unconcealment they cannot attain on their own. "Pure water had never been so transparent," he writes, and "the world-illuminating mirror has never furbished plants and flowers in that tone." Actual water, plants, or flowers, in other words, cannot express their qualities to the extent that these can become perceptible in art.

Mustafa Ali firmly embeds the artistic process in Sufi terminology, with Mani's burnishing of his wall an exact replication of Rumi's Greek artists polishing theirs, and the twice-mentioned "mirror" establishing art as a mirror of the divine absolute. Read in the light of Sufi philosophy, then, Mustafa Ali presents art—or, at the very least, great art—as a process of unconcealment that retrieves phenomena from their habitual invisibility and enables a direct apprehension of the absolute.

It is in this sense of unconcealment, rather than realism or verisimilitude, that the "life-giving" quality of miniature art needs to be understood. Read in this way, passages like the following couplet on Ibrahim Mirza by Qadi Ahmad make perfect sense:

Thanks to the mastery, the hair of his *qalam*
Gave life even to images of minerals.[66]

Ibrahim Mirza does not paint in such a realistic fashion that he makes even inanimate minerals "come to life." Rather, his art aids the minerals in their unconcealment by revealing their grounding in the ontological basis of all life.

## Sufism, Miniature Art, and Religious Literalism

The Sufi miniaturist, then, is not a fake "life-giver" who competes with the deity, a vulgar illusionist who pretends to divine powers by using artistic tricks to make his paintings seem literally alive. Rather, he acts as a conduit for the self-manifestation of the absolute, which achieves its unconcealment through his art. To think otherwise is a naïve misapprehension at best and a malicious misrepresentation at worst. Nonetheless, both miniature art and Sufism had to weather the harshest criticism. To the religious literalist, a miniaturist's depiction of phenomena smacks of idolatry, as does Ibn Arabi's assertion that "The perfect gnostic is one who regards every object of worship as a manifestation of God in which He is worshiped."[67]

Painters and Sufis alike were confronted with this accusation. Mustafa Ali gives the following account of Mani's execution: "The sages of the time envied his rise and pursued aggressively the rules of the arts of spying and hypocrisy. With their schism, the sages incriminated Mani."[68] Mani refuses to repent and "[does] not consider turning away from his conviction that a wicked picture [should be] discarded."[69] Whatever a "wicked picture" may be, Mani clearly rejects it and is condemned because of this rejection. Mustafa Ali, then, seems to turn Mani from a false prophet into a martyred opponent of idolatry: "it [is] decided that he be flayed and his skin be stuffed with straw and displayed."[70]

In his demise, Mustafa Ali's Mani resembles al-Hallaj (ca. 858-913), the most famous of Sufi martyrs, whose story is recounted by Fariduddin Attar in his *Memorial of the Saints*. Proclaiming "I am the Truth," al-Hallaj is accused by his literalist detractors of claiming to be God. Asked for his legal opinion, al-Hallaj's Sufi teacher Jonaid maintains "This is not the time for esoteric meanings" and supports the death sentence.[71] Al-Hallaj is beaten with sticks, crucified, and stoned; his hands and feet are severed; his eyes are gauged out; his tongue, ears, and nose are cut off; and he is beheaded. And still, "from each of his members [comes] the declaration, 'I am the Truth.'"[72] Finally, al-Hallaj's limbs are burned.

> From his ashes came the cry, "I am the Truth," even as in the time of his slaying every drop of blood as it trickled formed the word Allah. Dumbfounded, they cast his ashes into the Tigris. As they floated on the surface of the water, they continued to cry, "I am the Truth."[73]

In the light of Sufi philosophy, the insistent claim to divinity made by al-Hallaj himself, his limbs, his blood, and even his ashes, simply means that the absolute manifests itself even in the smallest particle of phenomenal existence—just as it does, as we have seen, in and through miniature art.

## 5. The Journey to the West

### *Miniature Art and Western Scholarship*

It is tragic but unsurprising that the miniature tradition did not survive the destruction of the court milieus that enabled its great flowering. As Michael Barry points out, the collapse of the Safavid Empire in the 18th century, followed by the final remnants of the Mughal Empire in the 19th century, spelled the end for miniature painting as a living art form.[1] Of course, this destruction went hand in hand with Western European cultural and political ascendancy over the geographies in question. As a result, it did not take long for miniature art to be "discovered," expropriated, and appropriated by persons and institutions from the West.

Barry outlines the process by which the first Western collectors such as Henri Vever, Victor Goloubew, and the Barons Edmond and Maurice de Rothshild started acquiring miniature art at the turn of the 20th century. The establishment of such collections was swiftly followed by a number of exhibitions that proved of fundamental importance to the development of 20th-century Western art: three exhibitions of Persian art at the Musée des arts décoratifs in Paris (1903, 1907, 1912) and a major exhibition of Eastern Islamic art in Munich (1910).[2] Some of the early Western collectors and popularizers of miniature painting were also among the first to write on the art form. Such was the case with Henri Vever and the Russian collector Ivan Stchoukine, "who fled to France after 1917 [and] became a leading scholar of Persian manuscript painting."[3]

However, as we have seen, this journey to the West was a violent—and violating—process which the artworks rarely survived intact. Barry describes the process in heartbreaking detail:

Paris dealers [...] cut up these manuscripts to sell their miniatures piecemeal, and each for high prices. [...] Profitable artistic massacres of this type continued to 1959, when US millionaire Arthur Houghton dismembered his own precious manuscript of a Book of Kings, which had once belonged to Shah Tahmasp, in order to sell its pictures, one by one, to dealers and collectors throughout North America and Europe.[4]

The isolated miniature painting came to be regarded as a visually pleasing and arresting artifact, while considerations of artistic context (the album) and cultural context (such as Sufi philosophy) fell by the wayside. In Barry's words, "Each illustrated Persian page, thus excised from its context, was offered for sheer aesthetic delight to Western amateurs: as an isolated art object, signifying nothing but its own color and design, and with nothing to impart but its charm."[5]

This superficial approach has also dominated Western scholarship on miniature art, which has been decidedly formalist and, in Barry's words, content "to map out the main historic lines of development, differentiate workshops and styles, and [...] identify the hand of individual masters."[6] Rather than attracting scholars of history and culture, let alone religion or philosophy, the field has largely been restricted to "art historians in the narrower sense: that is, to specialists preoccupied with style."[7] It is only at the turn of the 21st century that we witness the first Western scholarly efforts to approach the cultural and philosophical world of miniature art. And these efforts, as we will see below, can only be regarded as tentative first steps in the right direction.

One of the biggest obstacles to deeper scholarly engagement has been the convenient assumption of a categorical iconoclasm in Islam. If Islam is fundamentally opposed to the depiction of living beings, then miniature painting can only be, as Barry puts it, "a sort of pleasant but minor form of secular decoration—an historically aberrant aesthetic game of no intellectual importance and with no real spiritual role to play in a civilization otherwise sternly perceived as iconophobic."[8]

This "iconophobic fallacy" imprisons scholarship in a set of vicious circles. The first of these is on the theoretical level: miniature painting is seen as marginal because Islam is regarded as iconophobic, and Islam is regarded as iconophobic because miniature painting is seen as marginal. The second is on the practical level: since miniature painting is assumed not to relate fruitfully to history, religion, or philosophy, it can be studied by scholars with no knowledge in these fields; and since only such scholars study miniature painting, it ends up not relating to these fields.

To see how prevalent such attitudes are even in the 21st century, one need look no further than *On Islamic Art*, a 2001 study published by Mikhail Piotrovsky, Director of the Hermitage Museum in St. Petersburg. In this study, Piotrovsky blithely claims that "The sacred history of the Muslim may only be told in words. Thus it is accurate to state that Islamic art is in essence abstract and not figurative," and that "representations in Islamic art, both of animals and people, […] are never used for religious purposes and are generally completely secondary to the ornamentation."[9]

### Prophet Portraiture
We have seen above how, even if a miniature painting does not have an explicitly religious theme—its focus could be, for instance, on water or rocks—it can still refer the viewer back to underlying Sufi ideas. We have also seen how miniature paintings were deemed capable of directly manifesting the absolute rather than only serving as explanatory intermediaries between their beholders

and religious or philosophical worldviews. Nonetheless, the most sophisticated Western scholarship to date has only concerned itself with paintings that have unmistakable religious content.

Many miniature paintings feature scenes from the Quran, the lives of the prophet Muhammad and other prominent figures of Islamic history, or allegorical Sufi tales such as Attar's *Canticle of the Birds*. We also encounter more generically religious paintings, for instance of Sufis engaged in religious activity. Among this corpus of artworks, prophet portraiture has received the most attention, with art historians Christiane Gruber and David Roxburgh attempting to connect it to Sufi ideas.

Let us now take a look at these pioneering efforts, bearing in mind that they are not by scholars of philosophy—whether Sufi or Western—and tend to employ philosophical terminology in a somewhat haphazard way. In order to avoid terminological confusion, I will quote from these sources quite selectively and try to place their nonetheless valuable insights in the context of Sufi ontology as outlined above.

An artistic term commonly used by these sources is that of abstraction. However, when a miniature painting is described as "abstract" or "abstracted," we should not think of it in terms of, say, a Mondrian or Rothko painting that avoids figurative representation. Miniature paintings clearly represent human beings, animals, settings, and events, and are therefore figurative. They can only be called "abstract" in the sense that they do not use formal techniques of verisimilitude, such as perspectival depth, developed in Western painting. And even then, the term remains problematic since it assumes an established standard of verisimilitude that was subsequently "abstracted" or modified in favor of abstraction, as in Western art. This problematic assumption plagues Roxburgh's approach, to which I will turn now.

Roxburgh takes up Dust Mohammad's "Chest of Witnessing"—which we called a pictorial version of Ibn Arabi's *Bezels of Wisdom* above—to put forward his ideas about abstraction. He posits that the prophet portraits assembled in the Chest of Witnessing are "clearly distinct from their referents."[10] The portraits are "abstract" in the sense that they do not represent the actual features of the prophets as human beings. Rather, they are "copies after *acheiropoieta*, 'unmade' images fashioned by God, constituted at the beginning of time."[11]

But how did the artists distinguish embodied and "unmade"? A key part of the effort, so Roxburgh, was a refusal to differentiate physical features. Referring to an illustrated *Mirajnama* (the story of the prophet Muhammad's initiatory journey through paradise and hell), he points out that its paintings "eschew physiognomic peculiarities, resorting instead to typologies for angels and prophets."[12] The text of the *Mirajnama* supports this visual approach. When Muhammad meets the inhabitants of paradise, "they are all the same": as tall as Adam, as old as Jesus at his death, as handsome as the prophet Joseph, and so on. Further, "these perfect denizens of paradise have no unwanted body hair or beard."[13]

We could say, then, in Sufi ontological terms that miniature painting refused to differentiate prophets' physical features in an effort to expose them not simply as human beings, but as manifestations of the absolute. While this seems like a sound interpretation, Roxburgh does not leave it at that. He also views this "abstraction" as a formal attempt by the miniature tradition to distance itself from pre-Islamic painters like Mani. To Roxburgh, the particularity of Mani's art is merely its verisimilitude—in the Western sense, one assumes, though this remains unclear.

The "optical naturalism" of painters like Mani, so Roxburgh, "was a mode of visual trickery that misled viewers into equating what they saw with the real thing" and thus "confused viewers about the ontology of the image in front of them."[14] Without pointing to an actual tradition or concrete examples of paintings that had such an impact, Roxburgh in effect claims that viewers thought paintings in the style of Mani were "real." This confusion, with its accompanying risks of blasphemy and idolatry, was one that miniature art, according to Roxburgh, deliberately avoided.

> The specific formal language developed and applied by [miniature] artists distanced the total visual field of the two-dimensional painting from the sensation of actual vision. The abstract properties of paintings, and the habit of always placing limitations on the detail even in portraiture, which would seem to require it, eliminated the risk of reading the painting as real.[15]

It is a problematic assumption, to say the least, that at any point in history, viewers may have actually risked confusing a painting with the thing it depicts, and that artists tried to take measures to prevent this from happening. The broken pitchers in Mustafa Ali's story about Mani must be read in an allegorical, not a literal sense. And, as we saw earlier, Mehmed II had no concern that his realistic portrait by a Western artist could have been mistaken for himself. Therefore, I believe it wiser to avoid reading the stylistic features of miniature art as ways of eschewing realism, naturalism, or verisimilitude as understood in Western art.

Roxburgh is more effective when connecting miniature art to Sufi ontology, an approach also taken by Christiane Gruber:

> Methods of abstracting the prophetic body [...] were not just linked to prohibitory impulses; they could also elevate the viewer's vision

beyond the realm of form while simultaneously overcoming the disloyalty of mimetic depiction.[16]

Talking of a "realm of form" and its "beyond," Gruber employs a dualistic terminology that risks distorting Sufi ontology. Also, as I have argued, the differentiation between miniature art and "mimetic depiction" is unhelpful. But Gruber's main point that art may disrupt visual habits and enable a different kind of vision is well worth pursuing. Since the Sufi tradition regarded prophets themselves as "visual epiphanies of being [...] whose outer forms are only fully appreciable through the viewer's inner perception,"[17] prophet portraiture was a good venue to effect such a disruption.

The idea of "inner perception" needs some clarification. As Gruber puts it, Sufi thinkers "believed that real sight occurs not through ocular perception, but by means of the eye of the heart [...] or the eye of the soul."[18] This did not mean that visual perception should be abandoned altogether; rather, it should be redirected, refocused, and possibly reconditioned in order to enable an enhanced, more penetrating perception of the world. Prophet portraiture aimed at leading viewers to "experiential confrontations in pictorial form," namely confrontations between the beholder and the absolute.[19]

For concrete examples, Gruber turns to portraits of the prophet Muhammad. To Sufis, Gruber writes, "Muhammad's physical manifestation *in corpore* [was] an ongoing process of theophany, oftentimes beyond the visual reach of the believer's eyes."[20] In other words, Muhammad was seen as continuously oscillating between concealment and unconcealment. "In order to convey the antipodes of disclosure and exposure," Gruber maintains, miniature painters "experimented with various motifs and techniques."[21]

What, then, are these motifs and techniques? The earliest Muhammad portraits depict the prophet just like any other human being, but later paintings introduce two crucial visual innovations: a nimbus of fire (*nur Muhammad* or "Light of Muhammad") engulfing his face or entire body, and/or a veil obscuring his face. Gruber rejects the idea that painters employed such strategies to avoid criticism for depicting the prophet. Instead, she views the flaming nimbus and the facial veil as attempts to disclose Muhammad's physical presence while simultaneously concealing his immaterial substance, too brilliant to behold.[22]

To Gruber, both the flame and the veil stand for the aspect of divine self-manifestation that transcends ordinary perception: the flame is too bright to look at while the veil is impenetrable. However, if we argue, with Ibn Arabi, that all particulars are veils engaged in their own unveiling, concealing and unconcealing the absolute at the same time, the flame and the veil become one and the same: the veil is the only way for the flame to show itself.

These paintings aimed at nothing less than inducing a religious experience. This is especially clear for the "inscribed portraits," in which the veil covering the prophet's head is inscribed with the statement *Ya Muhammad* (O Muhammad).[23] Prompting the viewer "to call forth the Prophet through a combination of verbal prayers and mental picturing,"[24] such portraits functioned as meditative devices, enabling a visualization while also encouraging a vocalization and thereby combining visual and aural perception and vocal articulation in one meditative practice. They were, in Gruber's words, "purposefully destabilizing," demanding an "active negotiation" on the part of their viewers.[25]

Gruber refers back to Dust Mohammad for an exemplary viewer response to a prophet portrait. When the prophet's companions perusing the "Chest of Witnessing" finally reach the portrait of Muhammad, "teardrops streamed like stars from their eyes, and a longing for the Prophet was reborn in their hearts.".[26] In other words, their response is a combination of physical and spiritual elements, uniting body and mind in the Sufi manner.

The story of the "Chest of Witnessing" contains revealing parallels to the story of Sheikh San'an as found in Attar. As we saw above, this is the story of a Muslim sheikh who, just like the prophet's companions in Dust Mohammad, undertakes a journey to Constantinople. Once there, the Sheikh has a similar reaction to the sight of the Christian princess as the prophet's companions have to the portraits.

Both stories fix Constantinople, the city of the Christian "icon-worshippers," as the place where Muslims catch a glimpse of the absolute as manifest or as immanence. This immanence is encountered in the form of icons or potential idols, namely the princess in Attar and the prophet portraits in Dust Mohammad. Let us also remember here that Ibn Arabi holds up the gaze upon feminine beauty, as practiced by Sheikh San'an, as the "perfect contemplation of the Reality.".[27] It can be said, then, that Dust Mohammad makes the same case for portraiture: the contemplation of portraits is an efficacious practice for encountering the absolute as immanence.

In conclusion, then, we can say that Western scholarship on miniature painting today has started to recognize the religious context and efficacy of this art form, even if it still has not fully transcended the "iconophobic fallacy." That being said, scholarship is still limited to paintings with explicitly religious subject matter, suggesting that miniature art was, at best, a handy illustration of religious doctrine. However, as I have argued above, Sufi ontology regards miniature painting as a locus of divine self-manifestation, one that in and of itself, and regardless of its subject matter, can produce an encounter with the absolute.

## *Miniature Painting and Western Art*

Western artists of the early 20th century were just as fascinated by miniature painting as were European collectors, curators, and scholars. European techniques of art—and especially painting—were undergoing a profound transformation fueled by the arrival of shocking and unseen art from all over the world, including not only miniature painting but also "Japanese prints, Russian icons, and [...] West African sculpture."[28]

Henri Matisse, who was exposed to miniature painting during a visit to Moscow and through exhibitions in Munich and Paris, was among the most deeply affected.[29] Miniature painting enabled him to draw formal inspiration from a sophisticated tradition of art while breaking free from the limitations of his own artistic heritage. "My painting first observed the somber gamut of the masters whom I studied in the Louvre," the artist noted. "But then my palette cleared. This was the influence of the Impressionists, of the Neo-Impressionists, of Cézanne,[30] and of the Orientals,"[31] he said, adding that "one gives oneself all the more readily when one sees one's efforts confirmed by a tradition, however ancient that tradition might be. It helps you leap over the moat."[32]

Just like the Western scholars of his time, Matisse lacked the cultural and philosophical background to fully engage with this tradition. But unlike these scholars, he perceived the art on a visceral or even spiritual level: "I instinctively admired the Italian primitives in the Louvre, and after that, Oriental art, especially at the extraordinary exhibition in Munich,"[33] he said. "Persian miniatures [...] showed me all the possibilities offered by my sensations. [...] Revelation thus came to me from the East."[34]

According to Michael Barry, the miniaturists, with "their surface treatment of all planes alike while minimizing or ignoring attempts at perspective or illusory depth; their resort to non-naturalistic primary colors to heighten while harmonizing vivid contrasts of hues; and their purity of outline,"[35] were crucial to Matisse's efforts to overcome the verisimilitude of Western painting. As a direct influence, Barry lists the miniature painting *Prince Humay Meets the Princess Humayun of China in a Dream Garden* (ca. 1430), which Matisse saw at the Paris Exhibition of 1903:

> This painting [...] shows two princely lovers of ideal beauty suspended like colorful cut-out dolls against the equally flat background of an "orchard." [Costumes and flowers are] wrought in costly pigments of gold and silver, malachite and cinnabar, orpiment and powdered lapis lazuli rinsed in linseed oil [and] shine as if at brightest noontide, with all shadows banished and no diminishing of perspective, or indeed any illusionistic foreshortening, whatsoever.[36]

Miniature art influenced Matisse most strongly in his handling of color. "I felt a passion for color develop in me," he stated. "At that moment occurred the great exhibition of Mohammedan art."[37] The artist elaborates on his approach to color in the following passage:

> I use color as a means of expressing my emotion, and not as a transcription of nature. I use the most simple colors. I do not transform the colors myself, I allow the relation between the colors to take care of that. At stake for me is only to bring their (juxtaposed) contrasts to the fore, and so to stress them. Nothing prevents one from composing with only a few colors; just as music is built up solely of seven notes.[38]

What is the relationship between Matisse and miniature art when it comes to color? Clearly, the artist had no knowledge of how miniaturists thought about color and its deployment. Does this mean that he simply registered the appearance of color in miniature paintings and used it as a formal point of departure? Or might he have "understood" something about color in miniature art that went beneath the surface?

The importance of color in miniature art cannot be overstated. According to Barry, it is color that brings together the abstract and figurative elements of Bihzad's paintings in a coherent whole.[39] The functions of miniature color are explained by Welch as follows:

[Miniaturists] had to discover the properties of each hue both separately and in conjunction with all the rest, for in Iranian miniatures the palette not only forms a visual "chord," like a cluster of musical notes, but also can be enjoyed bit by bit. It is a great pleasure, for instance, to look at a miniature for the pattern of blues, reds, or whites alone.[40]

The colors and patterns described by Welch were not chosen at random but based on Sufi ideas. Barry draws our attention to the color scheme developed by the Sufi poet Nizami Ganjavi (1141-1209):

In his romance of spiritual initiation, the *Haft Paykar,* or "Seven Icons" ("Seven Beauties"), Nizami equated the Seven Colors of the universe with the seven metals, the world's seven climes, the seven planetary spheres, the seven days of the week, and the seven tinctures of the initiated soul.[41]

Nizami's scheme, however, was only one among many: there was no universally agreed-upon color scheme in which one color could carry only one meaning.[42] Had there been one, the result would have been a simple encoding and decoding of a philosophical/mystical message, a mechanical procedure that anyone familiar with the scheme could have carried out. Instead, it was up to the individual miniature painter to fashion the interplay of colors in such a way that a manifestation of the absolute emerged in their contemplation by the beholder.

Matisse, then, had no way of grasping the "letter" of miniaturists' color usage: he did not know any of their particular color schemes. But he very well grasped the "spirit" of this usage, in which the effect of color was not achieved by formulaic encoding and decoding, but in an intuitively determined relation between the colors.

## Artistic Transmission and Philosophical Equivalence

Curiously, Matisse's approach to miniature art mirrored that of the earliest miniaturists to their own primary fount of formal inspiration, namely Chinese art. Qadi Ahmad tells of an encounter between the Caliph Ali, the "patron saint" of miniaturists, and certain Chinese painters who, upon first hearing of the prophet Muhammad, decide to issue a challenge in the form of a painting:

> When the cycle of prophetic mission reached Muhammad,
> (And) he drew a line across all other faiths,
> The Chinese wrong-doers
> Traced the first images;
> Provocatively they embellished a page
> And asked the King of Prophets to produce something similar.
> It was not a page embellished,
> It looked like a tray filled with tulips and roses.
> From the very infidelity of their hearts,
> They carried the painting as a challenge
> To the Shah of Men, Ali.[43]

Here, we find the (mytho-)historical assertion that the Chinese were the first producers of images and the ones who transmitted this art to the Islamic world; an allusion to the compelling quality of their art; and an interpretation of the art as a challenge to Islam, which finds itself prompted to "produce something similar." The impertinence of the challenge lies not in the art of the Chinese, but in the "infidelity of their hearts" with which they aim to "provoke" Ali. Accordingly, his response does not take the form of an outright rejection.

> When the King of Holiness saw what they had painted,
> By miraculous power he took the *qalam* from them,
> And made an Islamic soul-ravishing tracing
> Which struck dumb the Chinese people.
> As the original fell into their hands,
> Their other images grew inferior.[44]

Ali, then, appropriates the tools (techniques) of Chinese art to produce a specimen that is both superior and somehow truer—it is described as "the original." Rather than setting up a contrast between, say, the idolatry of the Chinese painters and the aniconic religion of Islam, the story amounts to an acknowledgement of cultural influence—the art of painting was inherited from the Chinese—with an assertion that the source of influence has been superseded in terms of quality and authenticity.

This acknowledgment of influence echoes throughout the work of our authors, all of whom associate China with the archetypal painter-figure of Mani: Mustafa Ali calls him "the Chinese artist Mani,"[45] Qadi Ahmad mentions "the works of those gifted like Mani and of the wizards of China,"[46] and Dust Mohammad recounts that Mani regarded his own art as "equal to the Picture Gallery of China."[47] Finally, Rumi's story on Greek and Chinese art also approaches the "Chinese artists" with a skeptical reverence, presenting them as both formidably skilled and somehow spiritually deficient.

Michael Barry traces the formal influence of Chinese art on Miniature painting to Hulegu Khan's conquest of Baghdad in 1258 and the establishment of a political-cultural continuity between Beijing as the capital of the Mongol Empire and Tabriz as the center of the Ilkhanate, one of the empire's subdivisions. As Barry puts it, "Chinese aesthetics became the Mongol dynasty's aesthetics—the emblem of rule and legitimate world sovereignty, even in the eyes of the 'vassal Khans' in Tabriz.".[48] This is why, according to Barry, Dust Mohammad begins his history of miniature art with the painter Ahmad Musa, whose patron was Abu Sa'id Bahadur Khan, the last Ilkhanid ruler (r. 1317-1335).[49] Dust Mohammad writes that "the [style of] depiction that is now current was invented by him" and describes him as the master who "lifted the veil from the face of depiction.".[50]

"The style of these Chinese-influenced illustrations," Barry writes, "was so boldly different from anything painted before in Islam that a whole new kind of art did seem to be taking form in early fourteenth-century Tabriz.".[51] Islamic painters adopted not only techniques, such as "Chinese linear perspective [...] with no single vanishing point,"[52] but also a vocabulary of images: "Bihzad's trees, rocks, dragons, and clouds all ultimately derive from Chinese models.".[53] However, the original cultural significance of Chinese art was lost in transmission:

> Though bold, beautiful and original, the new Islamic art which arose under the impact of Chinese influence was the result of a complete misunderstanding of Chinese civilization by Muslim painters. The artists of Tabriz and Herat borrowed visual details from Chinese paintings—but utterly failed to grasp their spirit..[54]

A comparative assessment of Chinese and Islamic painting, including exactly what it was that did not survive the transmission, falls outside the scope of our study. However, Barry maintains that a "philosophical equivalence"[55] still obtains in the works of the greatest miniature painters such as Bihzad and their Chinese counterparts such as Shen Chou (1427-1506). Barry finds this equivalence in the notion of the "void," "the divine matrix of all being,"[56] or, in the ontological terminology we developed above, the absolute as unmanifested potentiality. Shared by Sufi and Taoist philosophy,[57] this notion was expressed in Chinese painting through whiteness—painters "lifted their brush and left their paper blank." In contrast, when Bihzad strove to express the same idea, he "charged his brush with ink and painted the heart of his composition in black."[58]

It is this kind of philosophical equivalence that I will be tracing from Ibn Arabi to Martin Heidegger and Maurice Merleau-Ponty. Western artists such as Henri Matisse may not have "understood" miniature art any better than miniaturists did their Chinese influences. But 20th-century philosophy of art, drawing on the work of such artists, showcases an affinity with the Sufi philosophy underlying miniature art that is simply too fruitful to ignore.

## 6. Phenomenology and Art:
## Balzac, Husserl, Heidegger

### *The Unknown Masterpiece*

The turn of the 20th century marked the end of an era for Western painting. As Gilles Deleuze puts it,

> Modern painting has a different relation to figuration or illustration than the painting of the past has. First, photography has taken over the illustrative and documentary role, so that modern painting no longer needs to fulfill this function, which still burdened earlier painters. Second, painting used to be conditioned by certain "religious possibilities" that still gave a pictorial meaning to figuration, whereas modern painting is an atheistic game..[1]

Hence, 20th-century Western artists' attraction to traditions that were unconcerned with verisimilitude—traditions that did not treat it like some universal principle one had to either adopt or reject, but that never tied artistic practice to the idea of verisimilitude in the first place. As Western art thus started parting ways with verisimilitude, it inspired philosophers to no longer view the work of art as a copy or representation of something "more real," but to approach it as a manifestation or unconcealment of being in its own right.

One of the first—and most lastingly influential—expressions of this philosophical approach is Honoré de Balzac's 1845 story, "The Unknown Masterpiece."[2] We might say that Balzac's protagonist, Frenhofer, creates the first modern painting half a century before the modern painters themselves. Both the painting in the story and the philosophy behind it are based on Frenhofer's central assertion that "the aim of art is not to copy."[3]

Over the years, the story came to inspire some of the most seminal Western painters and philosophers. Paul Cézanne, in one of his letters, flatly states "I am Frenhofer." Pablo Picasso painted his masterpiece *Guernica* in a location from the story, namely Porbus' studio in the Rue des Grands Augustins, Paris. And Maurice Merleau-Ponty takes Frenhofer as a starting point to explore not only Cézanne's work, but the art of painting in general.[4]

Frenhofer is a fictional 17th-century painter living in Paris. In the story's first half, he visits two admirers—the painters Nicolas Poussin and Porbus[5]—in the latter's studio, where he lectures them on art and being an artist as well as giving a "blood transfusion" to one of Porbus' paintings with a few brush strokes. Upon hearing that Frenhofer is in search of a new model for his next masterpiece,[6] Poussin and Porbus decide to present Poussin's lover Gillette to the master.

In the second half of the story, Frenhofer is the host while his two admirers and Gillette are his guests. He reveals to them the "unknown masterpiece" in which he has expended all his time and artistic powers. Poussin and Porbus are speechless: rather than the classical painting they had been expecting, they are met with a jumble of hectic colors and chaotic lines. They conclude that the master has finally lost his mind.

> "Do you see anything?" Poussin asked of Porbus.
> "No…do you?"
> "I see nothing."
> The two painters left the old man to his ecstasy, and tried to ascertain whether the light that fell upon the canvas had in some way neutralized all the effect for them. They moved to the right and left of the picture; they came in front, bending down and standing upright by turns.
> "Yes, yes, it is really canvas," said Frenhofer, who mistook the nature of this minute investigation.

"Look! the canvas is on a stretcher, here is the easel; indeed, here are my colors, my brushes," and he took up a brush and held it out to them, all unsuspicious of their thought.

"The old *lansquenet* is laughing at us," said Poussin, coming once more toward the supposed picture. "I can see nothing there but confused masses of color and a multitude of fantastical lines that go to make a dead wall of paint."

"We are mistaken, look!" said Porbus.

In a corner of the canvas, as they came nearer, they distinguished a bare foot emerging from the chaos of color, half-tints and vague shadows that made up a dim, formless fog. Its living delicate beauty held them spellbound. This fragment that had escaped an incomprehensible, slow, and gradual destruction seemed to them like the Parian marble torso of some Venus emerging from the ashes of a ruined town.

"There is a woman beneath," exclaimed Porbus, calling Poussin's attention to the coats of paint with which the old artist had overlaid and concealed his work in the quest of perfection..[7]

What the two friends view as a failure is in fact Frenhofer's true masterpiece. After the first shock, their not-yet-trained eyes slowly adjust to the painting. It tells them whether to approach or to distance themselves. It teaches them how it should be looked at. However, since it is ahead of its time, the two are unable to admire it. Frenhofer himself half expects his colleagues not to even recognize his work as a painting—as with Mani's prophetic scroll, which contains "various shapes that occur only in the mirror of the mind through the eye of imagination and that sit on the page of possibility in the visible world only with fantastic shapes."[8] And he is met with a similar level of incomprehension.

Unbeknownst even to himself, Frenhofer has become the first modern painter. He is on the way to dissolving the idea of "drawing" into its component parts and reassembling them in non-representational ways. However, he is so far ahead of his time that his project fills him with self-doubt. As Porbus puts it,

> Frenhofer is a passionate enthusiast, who sees above and beyond other painters. He has meditated profoundly on color, and the absolute truth of line; but by the way of much research he has come to doubt the very existence of the objects of his search. He says, in moments of despondency, that there is no such thing as drawing, and that by means of lines we can only reproduce geometrical figures.[9]

In Balzac, painting is no longer imitation, and the painter no longer an imitator. As Frenhofer says to his admirers, "The aim of art is not to copy nature, but to express it. You are not a servile copyist, but a poet!"[10] According to Frenhofer, form has a shifting nature that cannot be captured by imitation: "Form is a Proteus more intangible and more manifold than the Proteus of the legend; compelled, only after long wrestling, to stand forth manifest in his true aspect."[11] Here, we find an appreciation of painting as continuously coming into being, an appreciation that, as we shall see below, anticipates phenomenology and especially the work of Merleau-Ponty.

Poussin opines that "Everything combined to set the old man beyond the limits of human nature."[12] And indeed, there is something in-human about Frenhofer the genius, Frenhofer the ultimate artist. He takes artistic journeys that no painter has taken before and returns from them with artistic expressions that are utterly unfamiliar. He does not create objects pleasing to the eyes of accustomed beholders, but something which still waits to encounter its meaning, a meaning not yet established. His masterpiece is "unknown" since it has not yet acquired the meaning that culture will give to it.

## *The Phenomenological Epoché*

When the perceived shows itself to the perceiver, the result is not an unambiguous, clear apprehension; hence Poussin and Porbus' bewildered reaction to the "unknown masterpiece." But while works of art are clearly "special cases" in challenging perception, a "perfect" or unequivocal perception does not exist even in the case of more mundane things. As Ibn Arabi puts it in reverse, "The perfect gnostic is one who regards every object of worship as a manifestation of God in which He is worshiped. They call it a god, although its proper name might be stone, wood, animal, man, star, or angel."[13]

In phenomenology, Edmund Husserl talks of the inherent ambiguity of perception and the need to overcome ordinary, conditioned perception to find new ways of apprehending the perceived. Two core Husserlian concepts are "lack" and "excess," which can be ascribed to the perceiver and the perceived alike in the act of perception.

On the one hand, there is a lack in the perceived and an excess in the perceiver. The perceived never shows itself in its wholeness, but only through its parts, which Husserl calls "perspectival adumbrations."[14] Martin Heidegger illustrates this with the example of a chair: "When I see a sensibly perceptible object, this familiar chair here, I always see—understood as a particular way of seeing—only of the seat but not the lower surface."[15] I cannot perceive the chair in its totality, I can only see it from a certain point of view, and every time I change my point of view, I gain a part of the chair while losing another.

Nonetheless, I perform a process of completing the missing parts without actually seeing them and thereby arrive at the chair as "presumed in its *thing-totality*."[16] And this process points to the excess in the perceiver, whose intention always goes beyond that which she can actually see. As Husserl puts it:

I see this house, and it is the house in its sense. I am familiar with it. But then I can so regard the appearing side as if the house were entirely different from the rear—a large, deep structure, whereas it is shallow, and so on. I then have an image-object apprehension. [....] What kind of an apprehension is this? It is a modified apprehension as opposed to the perceptual apprehension that is still there, in conflict.[17]

The excess in the perceiver, then, leads to a mental manipulation of the perceived, with the perceived being apprehended in various ways that do not necessarily correspond to its actuality.

On the other hand, we can also assign excess to the perceived and lack to the perceiver. "The thing shows qualities and meanings," as Rudolf Bernet puts it, that "the perceiver did not expect, and its shining appearance carries a 'comet tail' of other possible appearances and other things possibly appearing."[18] To demonstrate, we can use the mundane example of a ladder used as a bookcase, a possibility not apparent until the perceiver oversteps the boundaries of his ordinary perception. This lack in the perceiver is mirrored by the excess in the perceived: there are more possibilities in a thing than ordinary perception suggests.

This is especially true in the case of art. To Heidegger, painting contains a special kind of excess that goes beyond ordinary things: "What is bodily perceived is the picture-thing itself, but this too is perceived in each instance in an aspect. To some extent, however, the perception of a picture-thing does not come to completion in the normal and natural perception of a picture."[19] This special excess in painting may be due to the fact that the painter, in Bernet's words, pursues "a perception of the world freed from the need of orientation, a non-instrumental relation to things, and a consideration of worldly events and situations for their own sake."[20]

None of this is meant to imply that ordinary perception is somehow wrong or undesirable; to the contrary, we need ordinary perception to function in our everyday lives.[21] However, it also blinds us to the richness of perceptual possibilities which will reveal itself to us if we manage to suspend ordinary perception. Such a suspension, as Bernet puts it, enables the perceiver "to see a web of interrelated appearances where others can only see solid things existing in and of themselves".[22]— or, as a Sufi might put it, to see with the "eye of the heart."[23] Husserl terms this suspension the phenomenological *epoché.* Bernet elaborates as follows:

> A *phenomenological epoché* [...] makes us aware of the fact that the perception of a visible thing necessarily includes an awareness of invisible aspects of the same thing. [....] In other words, without the awareness of the invisible sides, there are no adumbrations at all. [....] Thus, the not yet visible sides of the thing are not just perceived as possibly becoming visible in the further course of experience, they have a visibility of their own from the beginning.[24]

Just as the phenomenologist aims for the phenomenological *epoché,* the painter aims for a "pictorial epoché," to discover, in Bernet's words, "the coming forth or 'birth' of both things and the world out of a manifold of ever-changing appearances."[25] To achieve this, the painter "will have to overcome a schematic seeing of familiar shapes and their distribution in a geometrical space in order to perceive colors just as colors, light and shadows, or empty spaces."[26] And if the pictorial *epoché* is indeed achieved, the result will be paintings that "change our way of perceiving real things, and [...] make us aware of unknown dimensions of our own mind."[27] The change that Bernet has in mind is nothing short of revolutionary:

> Forms will dissolve in shapes, shapes will become patches of color, patches of color will assemble and separate in a ballet dance to a yet unheard musical rhythm. Thus, transformed in her way of seeing the world by her seeing of art, she [the beholder] also sees painted works of art differently. Sensitive to an overall proximity between the visible and the invisible, when visiting an art museum, she will pass from the contemplation of figurative paintings to the contemplation of abstract paintings without noticing the difference.[28]

It is hard to overlook the parallels between the phenomenological approach to perception and that outlined by Ibn Arabi. The Sufi takes up the inextricable interwovenness of the visible and the invisible when he describes the absolute as "nothing other than what comes out outwardly, whereas in the very moment of coming out outwardly it is what conceals itself inwardly."[29] He expresses the limits of "schematic" thinking and seeing when he says that "the intellect restricts and seeks to define the truth within a particular qualification, while in fact the Reality does not admit of such a limitation."[30] And his notion of the "Breath of the Merciful," with its view of creation as a constantly recurring process of rebirth, anticipates the phenomenological notion of being as a perpetual process of "birth" or "coming forth."

Let me repeat that I am not arguing for a one-to-one overlap between phenomenological and Sufi thought. For instance, the phenomenological approach to perception and art does not contain the spiritual/moral dimension that, in Sufi thought, must accompany any attempt at perception of the absolute. What to phenomenologists consists of a sheer method, or technique, of apprehending the perceptible world is, to Sufi thinkers, part of a holistic approach that intertwines religious, ethical, sensory, and many other dimensions.[31] Nonetheless, both forms of thought converge on an understanding of being as a perpetual process of coming-into-being that cannot be apprehended by conceptual means. Further, both sides grant a privileged position to painting as a non-conceptual practice that can capture and convey this coming-into-being.[32]

## Peeling off the Layers

Husserl's thoughts on the phenomenological *epoché* are echoed by Martin Heidegger in his essay, "The Origin of the Work of Art." There is an obscured, primordial level of being to be found in a work of art, Heidegger writes, and Western theories of art, whether traditional or modern, are unable to reach this level. Instead, he argues, all they do is imprison the work of art in a conceptual framework based on dichotomies such as object-subject, form-matter, or *substantia et accidens*. Instead of such a metaphysically invested aesthetics, Heidegger proposes an ontological approach to art based on the concept of truth as *aletheia*—that is to say, truth as the unconcealment of being.

To Heidegger, one never approaches a work of art naïvely. Even before encountering the work itself, one engages with the preconceptions surrounding it, instigated by anything from trivia to philosophy. It is these preconceptions that shape our ordinary perception—in Ibn Arabi's words, "The intellect restricts and seeks to define the truth within a particular qualification." As we have seen, the Sufi goes on to maintain that "in fact the Reality does not admit of such a limitation,"[33] and the same resistance of being to conceptual apprehension is also maintained by Heidegger. In his phenomenology, every showing is a self-showing, and the moment one imposes certain preconceptions on beings, one stops them from showing themselves.

Heidegger begins by mapping out the conceptual constructs that surround the work of art and conceal it from our sight. He then tries to peel these preconceptions off the work, "to remove the work from all relations to anything other than itself in order to let it stand on its own and for itself alone."[34] This, he maintains, is the only way to approach the work in its "immediate and complete reality."[35] Heidegger's method may be compared to an archaeological excavation of an artifact buried underground. His first step is a preliminary field excursion, investigating the different layers covering the work. His second step is to remove the layers one by one so that the work can reveal itself. As with the phenomenological *epoché*, the question here is not to declare these "ordinary" approaches to art valueless or "incorrect." As Mark Sinclair puts it,

> The long history of traditional approaches to art [...] is no mere aberration since it is always possible to locate the truth or correctness of these concepts in the work. Yet, what Heidegger terms the "fatality" of this history would consist in the fact that the self-evidence of such approaches only veils a more original apprehension.[36]

There are three main preconceptions, Heidegger writes, that reduce the work of art to the conceptual level. The first of these is the dichotomy of *substantia* and *accidens*: "It is generally held that the definition of the thingness of the thing in terms of substance and accidents appears to capture our natural view of things."[37] This preconception, to Heidegger, is embedded in the structure of language itself:

> The simple declarative sentence consists of a subject–the Latin translation, and that means transformation,[38] of *hypokeimenon*–and predicate, which expresses the thing's characteristics. Who would dare to threaten this simple and fundamental relationship between thing and sentence, between the structure of the sentence and the structure of the thing?[39]

Joseph Kockelmans, following Heidegger, traces the subject-predicate dichotomy to the Ancient Greeks:

> For them the core of the thing [the *hypokeimenon*] was something lying on the ground, something that is always already present. On the other hand, they called the characteristics the *sumbebekota*, that which always turns up along with the core as soon as the latter appears; it is that which occurs together with the core.[40]

It follows that the work of art, just like all other things, is made up of two parts, substance and properties, which reduces it to the bearer of certain characteristics. But to Heidegger, "the thing is not merely a collection of characteristics, and neither is it the aggregate of those properties through which the collection arises."[41] Viewing the artwork through such a theoretical framework already bars one from apprehending its immediate reality.

The second preconception is that of the artwork as *aistheton*, or as the monolithic unity of its manifold constituents given to the senses:

> In what the senses of sight, hearing, and touch bring to us, in the sensations of color, sound, roughness, and hardness, things move us bodily, in a quite literal sense. The thing is that *aistheton*, that which, in the senses belonging to sensibility, is perceptible by means of sensations.[42]

Approaching the artwork as *aistheton* reduces it to a unity of its manifold sensory effects. This is the polar opposite of the first preconception, where the artwork is reduced to a bearer of multiple characteristics. As Heidegger puts it, "the first interpretation of the thing holds it, as it were, too far away from the body, the second brings it too close."[43]

To Heidegger, aesthetics is "the way of inquiring into art and the beautiful on the basis of the state of feeling in enjoyers and producers."[44] Such an approach is not grounded in the artwork itself, investigating it only "from the point of view of expression and impression,"[45] namely the expression aimed at by its "producers" and the impressions ensuing in its "enjoyers."[46] As Karsten Harries puts it, "what is enjoyed is not so much the work of art, as the occasioned experience or state of mind. Aesthetic enjoyment is fundamentally self-enjoyment."[47]

The aesthetic tendency, Heidegger writes, "is old, just as old as meditation on art and the beautiful in Western thought."[48] Here, Heidegger is referring to Plato as the intellectual precursor of the Cartesian dualism that makes the aesthetic approach possible.[49] "The artwork is posited as the 'object' for a 'subject,' and this subject-object relation, specifically as a relation of feeling, is definitive for aesthetic consideration."[50] The main issue here is not aesthetics' neglect of the "object" (work of art) in favor of the "subject" (artist or viewer) but rather the dichotomy between subject and object itself. In Harries' words,

> The Cartesian world-picture assumes an "I" placed before and thus outside it. The Cartesian *res cogitans* has thus no place in the world whose essence Descartes determines as *res extensa*. The subject has fallen, had to fall out of the world so understood.[51]

As we already know, the subject-object dichotomy is a major point of irritation not just for Heidegger but also for Ibn Arabi, according to whom "positing something other than what is looked on, thus establishing a relation between two things, the observer and the thing observed, nulli[fies] the Unity"[52] sought after in Sufism.

The third preconception views the artwork in terms of matter and form. This is the thickest layer to cover the work of art, and also the closest, since to Heidegger, it is the most widespread and apparently self-evident of all three. The distinction of matter and form (*hule* and *morphe* in Greek terminology) can be traced back to Plato, for whom, in Kockelmans' words, "what limits is form, and what is limited is matter."[53] In this preconception, an artwork contains two competing forces, one passive, the other active. On the one hand, there is irrational, illogical matter; on the other, there is the rational, meaningful form which a forming agent bestows upon it.

Now, just as Ibn Arabi views our ordinary perception like a dream that, interpreted correctly, can set us on the right path to the absolute, I would argue that Heidegger also views the preconceptions as potential clues that can lead us to the authentic truth of an artwork. And since the matter-form dichotomy presents the thickest layer covering the work, it also potentially carries the most traces of an originary experience. So, rather than simply dismiss it, Heidegger tries to unlock this third preconception by way of such an experience.

### The Peasant Shoes

"What art may be," Heidegger writes in "The Origin of the Work of Art," "is one of the questions to which this essay offers no answer."[54] His intention is not to produce a new theory of art—in other words, another layer that would cover the work.[55] Instead, what Heidegger offers us is a phenomenological description based on a direct engagement with a particular work of art:[56] a pair of peasant shoes by Van Gogh.[57]

> From the dark opening of the worn insides of the shoes the toilsome tread of the worker stares forth. In the stiffly rugged heaviness of the shoes there is the accumulated tenacity of her slow trudge through the far-spreading and ever-uniform furrows of the field swept by a raw

wind. On the leather lie the dampness and richness of the soil. Under the soles slides the loneliness of the field-path as evening falls. In the shoes vibrates the silent call of the earth, its quiet gift of the ripening grain and its unexplained self-refusal in the fallow desolation of the wintry field. This equipment is pervaded by uncomplaining anxiety as to the certainty of bread, the wordless joy of having once more withstood want, the trembling before the impending childbed and shivering at the surrounding menace of death. The equipment belongs to the earth and it is protected in the world of the peasant woman. From out of this protected belonging the equipment itself rises to its resting-within-itself.[58]

Heidegger approaches the dichotomy of matter and form through the notions of earth and world, which, as Sinclair explains, "are not themselves things, but two ontological differentials, two aspects of the being of beings."[59] In trying to better understand earth and world, a good way to start is with that which unites them: the notion of equipment. Pieces of equipment, as Heidegger explains in *Being and Time*, are not "objects for knowing the 'world' theoretically; they are simply what gets used, what gets produced, and so forth."[60] Van Gogh's painting gives us the equipmentality of the shoes in their wear and tear, their having-been-usedness. The peasant woman wears the shoes and thus uses them like any other tool or equipment at her disposal. When worn by her in the fields, the shoes are what they are.

Equipment belongs to the earth, "on which man bases his dwelling" and "in which the arising of everything that arises is brought back—as, indeed, the very thing that is—and sheltered. In the things that arise the earth presences as the protecting one."[61] In the case of the peasant woman, earth is not simply the materiality of the equipment she uses, but also the field, the land upon which she lives and works. However, the pair of shoes is also preserved in the world of the peasant woman, implying the whole context of meaningful relations that forms her experience as a human being. In Heidegger's words,

> World is not a mere collection of things—countable and uncountable, known and unknown—that are present at hand. Neither is world a merely imaginary framework added by our representation of the sum of things that are present. World worlds, and is more fully in being than all those tangible and perceptible things in the midst of which we take ourselves to be at home. World is never an object that stands before us and can be looked at. World is that always-nonobjectual to which we are subject as long as the paths of birth and death, blessing and curse, keep us transported into being.[62]

Earth and world are simultaneously present for the peasant woman only in the reliability of equipment. As Heidegger puts it, "In virtue of this reliability the peasant woman is admitted into the silent call of the earth; in virtue of the reliability of the equipment she is certain of her world."[63]

The notion of reliability goes beyond the mere usefulness of the shoes. For the peasant woman, using the shoes means depending on them. But as she uses them, they sustain an increasing amount of damage, clearly evinced by the deformity of the shoes in the painting: "The individual piece of equipment becomes worn out and used up. But also, customary usage itself falls into disuse, becomes ground down and merely habitual. In this way equipmental being withers away, sinks to the level of mere equipment."[64]

The usefulness of the shoes, then, is merely the temporary manifestation, in this particular piece of equipment, of the deeper notion of reliability that is tied up with the idea of equipment itself.[65] This notion of reliability is so ingrained that the peasant woman might hardly even notice the shoes' role in her life, yet would still know, simply by virtue of using them, that which we only come to realize about them in the painting. Were the shoes to fall apart, their reliability would become immediately apparent to her because of its absence in this particular pair of shoes.

Still, as she wears them in the field, the peasant woman's knowledge of the shoes remains "wordless," as Harries puts it. [66] "The equipmentality of equipment," Harries writes, "did not arrive at its appearance in the peasant woman's wordless knowledge of her shoes. She was too secure and embedded in her world for her shoes to yield such an appearance. Their very reliability precluded it.". [67] Just as with the pen and paper that we forget about in the act of writing with them, and that we only notice if we run out of ink, the thing disappears in its use.

To perceive a thing's unconcealment, we need a certain distance from it and its function. Art, so Heidegger, provides us with this distance. A work of art acts like an interruption. It shakes the ground on which we stand and forces us to think about what we take for granted, it makes the invisible visible—the shoes to the peasant, the pen to the writer. We start to see the thing, not from a different perspective, but as if for the first time, without reducing it to a function, without pre-givens, presuppositions, or concepts.

When Mustafa Ali informs us that "pure water had never been so transparent" as in a painting by Mani, [68] or when Qadi Ahmad tells us that Ibrahim Mirza's paintings "gave life even to images of minerals,". [69] I read them as referring to the same process outlined by Heidegger, whereby the artwork enables an apprehension of the thing not accessible through the thing itself. Traits like the particular transparency of water escape the casual observer because of her habitual acquaintance with things, while art allows these traits to manifest as if observed for the first time. And it is this fresh manifestation that gives them "life."

## *Earth, World, and Strife*

Let us now return to the notions of earth and world: how do they relate to art, and how do they take us beyond the matter-form dichotomy towards a more primordial experience? According to Heidegger, the artwork enables us to apprehend the relationship between earth and world. "The work holds open the open of a world,"[70] Heidegger says, while at the same time, "the work moves the earth into the open of a world and holds it there."[71]

"Far from being a mere matter lacking a form," Sinclair explains, "earth is already the emerging of latent and present figures and shapes."[72] The bronze already carries Rodin's *Thinker* within itself as a potentiality, and Michelangelo's *David* is already a possibility within the marble. But earth, to Heidegger, "is essentially self-secluding,"[73] which means that an artwork cannot simply drag it out into the open; it needs to "bring [earth] into the open *as* the self-secluding."[74] Colors contain the potential to become miniature paintings, while through miniature paintings, they come into their own and become visible in a specific way even as they seclude themselves in the painting's "figures and shapes."

While the work of art lets earth be earth without reducing it to anything other than itself, there are other circumstances that preclude such an unconcealment. For one, the earthly character of a thing can disappear into its usefulness. Thus, equipment tends to reduce materiality to usefulness and thereby almost covers up its own earthly aspect. In a hammer, for instance, the wood of the handle becomes subsumed in the handle's functionality.

The second way of "not letting earth be earth" is to force it into presence via scientific investigation. Heidegger gives the example of color, which "shines and wants only to shine. If we try to make it comprehensible by analyzing it into numbers of oscillations it is gone. It shows itself only when it remains undisclosed and unexplained."[75] The Sufi color schemes we mentioned above tie in perfectly with this example: a consistent scheme applied across all miniature paintings would reduce coloration to a mere cognitive game rather than opening up the primordial potentiality realized by a Matisse. Through such an analytical approach, as Heidegger puts it in *Being and Time*, "everything primordial gets glossed over as something long familiar. Everything gained by a struggle becomes just something to be manipulated. Every mystery loses its power."[76]

Let us now turn to the notion of world. "The stone is world-less," Heidegger tells us. "The peasant woman, by contrast, possesses a world."[77] However, this is neither a world constructed by her, nor one to which she stands opposed as a Cartesian subject. Instead, as Sinclair puts it, world is "an essential aspect of the being of *Dasein* as a being-in-the-world."[78] The peasant woman is a particular *Dasein* (literally, "being-there"), a being-in-the-world that inhabits the world into which she is thrown.

This leads us to the second Heideggerian usage of world, which goes beyond the particular individual to cover an epoch. According to Sinclair, "There is a 'worlding' of the world that is given to the being-in-the-world that we are, and in its different epochal formations world is the web of 'paths and relations' within which individuals always and already find themselves."[79] Both earth and world are equally blind forces of coming-into-being; "the idea of world," Sinclair writes, "delimits and transcends traditional determinations of the intelligible."[80] Returning to art, then, it is clear that the worldly element of the work cannot simply be a force that shapes earth according to a pre-given intellectual agenda.[81]

It might be tempting to talk of a mutual relationship between earth and world, but even the idea of such a mutuality or *betweenness* introduces a separation that is impermissible to

Heidegger. Earth and world co-exist. As Kockelmans puts it, "The earth cannot be without the open of the world, if it is to appear as earth in the liberated surge of its self-seclusion. On the other hand, the world cannot rise above the earth and freely float away from it, if (as the governing path of all destiny) it is to ground itself on a resolute foundation."[82]

This might sound as if earth provides an ontological ground on which world establishes itself, but that would imply a hierarchical relationship contrary to Heidegger's intentions. There is neither a horizontal nor vertical relationship—earth and world are not above and below each other, and neither are they next to each other. While they can be distinguished conceptually, they are interwoven in a way that makes it impossible to clinically detach earthly aspects of a thing from its worldly aspects. It is perhaps this fraught interwovenness that leads Heidegger to describe the dynamics between earth and world not in terms of harmony, but of strife.

Ibn Arabi, as we have seen above, views the perceptible world of particulars (the cosmos) as both a veiling and an unveiling of the absolute, which is involved in a perpetual process of simultaneous self-concealment and self-disclosure. In his words, "The Absolute [....] is nothing other than what comes out outwardly, whereas in the very moment of coming out outwardly it is what conceals itself inwardly."[83] Like Heidegger, Ibn Arabi understands this veiling-unveiling process in terms of strife: "The act of creation constitutes an imbalance in Nature that might be called a deviation or alteration. [....] Harmony and equilibrium are everywhere sought, but never achieved."[84]

## Strife in the Work of Art

According to Heidegger, in a work of art, there is an ongoing strife between earth and world. Two mutually constitutive forces with self-concealing and self-unconcealing tendencies, earth and world bring each other out in the artwork, leaving it in a state of extreme tension. "The work," as Kockelmans puts it, "is the instigation of the striving. And work never puts an end to the strife, but makes certain that the strife remains strife."[85] For an example, we can turn to the miniature tradition of prophet portraiture, where the simultaneous process of concealment and unconcealment expressed in the prophet's appearance resulted in works of art that Gruber describes as "purposefully destabilizing."[86]

Heidegger himself illustrates the strife between earth and world in the work of art through his famous example of the Greek temple. The stone out of which the temple emerges shows itself through the temple. However, the stone is not the only earthly element revealed through the work; its environment or milieu, consisting of air, light, the ground beneath the temple, and so on, equally becomes present:

> Standing there, the building rests on the rocky ground. This resting of the work draws out of the rock the darkness of its unstructured yet unforced support. Standing there, the building holds its place against the storm tagging above it and so first makes the storm visible in its violence. The gleam and luster of the stone, though apparently there only by the grace of the sun, in fact first brings forth the light of day, the breadth of the sky, the darkness of night. The temple's firm towering makes visible the invisible space of the air.[87]

Earth, as it shows itself through the work of art, is not the mere materiality of the work but being as a whole. And world is revealed in the work in a similar way:

> It is the temple work that first structures and simultaneously gathers around itself the unity of those paths and relations in which birth and

death, disaster and blessing, victory and disgrace, endurance and decline acquire for the human being the shape of its destiny.[88]

The temple, then, does not only gather earth and world, letting both reveal themselves in their strife with each other. It also exposes the strife that earth and world experience within themselves. Although earth has a self-concealing tendency, the work reveals there is a dynamic of self-concealing *and* self-unconcealing within that tendency itself. And the work reveals the same dynamic within the world's tendency towards self-unconcealing. Accomplishing all this at once, the work performs a gathering of that which is ungatherable by any other means.

Inside the temple, it is the statue of the deity that exemplifies the gathering of earth and world. This statue, to Heidegger, is not a representation of something other than itself: "The work is not a portrait intended to make it easier to recognize what the god looks like. It is, rather, a work which allows the god himself to presence and *is*, therefore, the god himself"[89]—or, as Ibn Arabi puts it, "The perfect gnostic is one who regards every object of worship as a manifestation of God in which He is worshiped."[90]

For the worshiper entering the temple, then, there is no clear line separating the idea and the materiality of the deity. Where does the materiality end and the idea begin? Or, in other words, what is earth and what world in a statue of the god? The statue gathers both and prohibits a clear distinction.

## The End of the World

"Art," Sinclair writes, "is not to be understood as an expression of an age, and the temple does not merely, as might also be said, give form to Greek culture. On the contrary, as an *original* work it achieves, establishes and opens this culture itself."[91] The entire city gathers around the temple; the entirety of life is lived through, around, and within it. The work of art, then, is not a representation of the world, but the center of the world. But what happens when that world comes to an end?

Heidegger's world is historical, and the work of art is an event in which all beings of a particular historical period reveal themselves. The temple is such a work only as long as it remains a gathering place as described above. But once it becomes something else, for instance an object to be sold, visited, or photographed, it is displaced. And the displacement of the work is inseparable from the displacement of its world. As Heidegger puts it,

> Even when we try to cancel or avoid such displacement of the work—by, for example, visiting the temple at its site in Paestum or Bamberg cathedral in its square—the world of the work that stands there has disintegrated.[92]

A similar thought is expressed by Wassily Kandinsky:

> Every work of art is the child of its time, often it is the mother of our emotions. Thus, every period of culture produces its own art, which can never be repeated. Any attempt to give new life to the artistic principles of the past can at best only result in a work of art that resembles a stillborn child. For example, it is impossible for our inner lives, our feelings, to be like those of the ancient Greeks.[93]

To Heidegger, there is no timeless world, idea, or phenomenon. Being is (in) time; it is historical being. In Sinclair's words,

> Philosophy is historical in its essence, it thinks from within history and cannot legitimately stake a claim to an eternal truth that would have descended from an otherworldly sphere, because Heidegger argues

that the human being, as what he terms *Dasein*, is a being that is in its essence time. [94]

Rejecting Hegelian trajectories of progress, Heidegger proposes a historicity of being that is not embedded in a teleological narrative. His individual and cultural worlds, intertwined with each other, constitute epochs, and works of art are immersed in these epochs. They do not inhabit a special place outside of space and time in which they can be objectively identified as works of art. The moment the world outside/inside the temple is "worn out" and comes to an end, the statue becomes a statue and is no longer a god.

This means even the strife between earth and world is not outside time. When an epoch is over, its uniquely established strife between earth and world disintegrates as well. Even though the Greek temple may still astonish us today, it does not institute a worldview, nor does it establish, preserve, or transform a community. Nonetheless, when we visit the temple today, we may still experience its encapsulation of Greek culture with its literature, art, philosophy, technology, religion, customs, and so on. In this sense, the Greek temple may be called, in Heideggerian terms, a work of "great art." Kockelmans explains the notion as follows:

"Great art" refers to those works that were produced in Greece, Rome, and the Middle Ages, and which are such that there is today common agreement on their artistic status. Great art implies the totality of all art works, made before the time in which the fine arts came to the fore as such, before the time in which artists began to claim to have a special "vocation" not to be shared with the mere craftsmen, and before works were preserved, exhibited in museums and exhibitions, dramas and musical works reproduced time and again in special auditoriums, etc. [95]

The development outlined by Kockelmans ties in with Heidegger's thoughts on aesthetics:

> Almost as soon as specialized thinking about art and the artist began, such reflections were referred to as "aesthetic." Aesthetics treated the artwork as an object, as indeed an object of aesthesis, of sensory apprehension in a broad sense. These days, such apprehension is called an "experience." The way in which man experiences art is supposed to inform us about its essential nature. Experience is the standard-giving source not only for the appreciation and enjoyment of art but also for its creation. Everything is experience. But perhaps experience is the element in which art dies. This dying proceeds so slowly that it takes several centuries.[96]

Once a work of art is turned into an aesthetic object and appropriated by the art industry, it loses its vitality—after all, it was not a "work of art" in the aesthetic sense for the people who originally interacted with it.[97] With its world at an end and its incorporation into the project of aesthetics, the "great work of art" perhaps still remains relevant, but is no longer "great" in Heidegger's sense. Clearly, this process also relates to the miniature album and its changing fortunes across time. While I will explore this relation more extensively later, we may maintain for now that the fate of the miniature album in the hands of Western collectors and scholars was not unlike that of the religious edifices Heidegger describes as having become mere sites of tourism.[98]

### The Fundamental Question

"There is nothing surrounding this pair of peasant shoes".[99]—this is the point, I would argue, where Heidegger hopes to arrive after peeling away all the layers surrounding the artwork. There is "nothing," no object or idea, left to represent; there is "nothing," no preconception, to cover up the painting. "A pair of shoes and nothing more. And yet."[100] Heidegger's "yet" points to what we might encounter amidst this "nothing." As he puts it in *Introduction to Metaphysics*:

> A painting by Van Gogh: a pair of sturdy peasant shoes, nothing else. The picture really represents nothing. Yet you are alone at once with what is there, as if you yourself were heading homeward from the field on a late autumn evening, tired, with your hoe, as the last potato fires smolder out.[101]

It is this "nothing" that Heidegger wants us to encounter via the work of art, an encounter that leads us straight to the fundamental question of ontology as formulated by Heidegger in the same work: "why is there something rather than nothing?"[102] The question pertains not to this or that being, or to all beings considered as a whole, but to the possibility of beings as such. Nothing turns out to be an indispensable element of the question since it prevents us from beginning directly with beings as unquestionably given and confronts the possibility of being with the possibility of not being.[103]

Just like the work of art, Heidegger's fundamental question enables us to abandon the solid ground of preconceptions in order to question the ground itself: "From what ground do beings come? On what ground do beings stand? To what ground do beings go?"[104] But the abandonment of ostensibly solid ground entails a leap, and it is this concept of the originary leap (*Ur-sprung*) that ties together Heidegger's thinking on being and art. The title of Heidegger's work, "The Origin of the Work of Art," contains the same concept of *Ursprung* (translated here as "origin"). Heidegger discusses this leap in *Introduction to Metaphysics*:

The leap [*Sprung*] of this questioning attains its own ground by leaping, performs it in leaping. According to the genuine meaning of the word, we call such a leap that attains itself as ground by leaping an originary leap [*Ur-sprung*]: an attaining-the-ground-by-leaping. Because the question "Why is there something rather than nothing?" attains the ground for all genuine questioning by leaping and is thus an originary leap, we must recognize it as the most originary [*ursprünglich*] of questions.[105]

What makes us take the leap? I think the answer is "nothing" itself, i.e., not-being, hiddenness, concealment. It is not the apparent, but the concealed that prompts us to go beyond the familiar and toward the strange. This is certainly the case in Ibn Arabi's ontology, in which the absolute desires to "reveal to Him[self] His own mystery"[106] and does so via self-manifestation, thereby taking a leap into "existence,"[107] a leap that, in Heidegger's parlance, attains its own ground.

### Phusis as Aletheia

Heidegger mirrors Ibn Arabi's skepticism towards the restrictive and particularizing operations of the intellect. It is not by gathering information, or by completing a process of instruction, that one "knows," i.e., answers the fundamental question. Rather, Heidegger regards knowledge as a certain disposition towards learning. Knowledge is the ability to learn, and the ability to learn presupposes the ability to question. Questioning, in turn, means letting beings unconceal themselves as they are—"the relation to Being is letting"[108]—and facing the openness of being unconcealed and kept open by questioning, thus remaining at a point where one can continually learn.[109]

This learning posture is necessitated by Heidegger's particular understanding of being, one which he derives from the

Greek word *phusis.*[110] Heidegger connects *phusis* to his notion of earth:

> Early on, the Greeks called this coming forth and rising up in itself and in all things *phusis*. At the same time *phusis* lights up that on which man bases his dwelling. We call this the earth. [....] Earth is that in which the arising of everything that arises is brought back—as, indeed, the very thing that it is—and sheltered. In the things that arise the earth presences as the protecting one.[111]

This unconcealment is experienced everywhere, especially within humans' immediate envelopment, i.e., nature. But nature itself is only possible due to something more primordial and fundamental, namely *phusis* itself. Therefore, *phusis* may not be reduced to nature, as the Romans did, Heidegger claims, when they translated *phusis* as *natura.*[112] To the Greeks, *phusis* first came to disclose itself "on the basis of a fundamental experience of being in poetry and thought," not in natural processes.[113]

Heidegger's *phusis* is that which "emerges from itself [...], the unfolding that opens itself up, the coming-into-appearance in such unfolding, and holding itself and persisting in appearance— in short, the emerging-abiding sway."[114] Emerging and abiding are not just ordinary processes that beings are observed to undergo among others—it is through the very process of emerging-abiding sway that beings become and remain observable in the first place.[115]

The connection between emerging and abiding helps us avoid an understanding of being as unchanging. "Being essentially unfolds as *phusis*,"[116] Heidegger writes, and *phusis* is something dynamic, it is a constant movement, it is in flux. This is a radical reimagining of the concept of being; in Charles Guignon's words, Heidegger offers:

a way of replacing the substance ontology that dominates Western thought with an alternative understanding of Being, an understanding that emphasizes the way beings show up in (and as) an unfolding happening or event.[117]

According to Heidegger, being has an essential relation not only to *becoming*, but also to *appearing*.[118]

> The emerging sway is an appearing. As such, it makes manifest. This already implies that being, appearing, is letting-step-forth from concealment. Insofar as a being as such is, it places itself into and stands in unconcealment, *aletheia*. [...] For the Greek essence of truth is possible only together with the Greek essence of being as *phusis*. On the grounds of the unique essential relation between *phusis* and *aletheia*, the Greeks could say: beings as beings are true. The true as such is in being. [....] Truth, as un-concealment, is not an addendum to being.[119]

In such disclosure, a being *is* in truth and emerges as unconcealment, or *aletheia*.[120] While *aletheia* broadly means "truth," the word contains a double negative: the prefix *a-* can mean "not," "without," "lack of," or "absence of," while *-letheia* derives from *lethe*, a state of being hidden or concealed. *A-letheia* thus denotes coming out of concealment, or becoming evident, unconcealed, unveiled. As unconcealment through the appearing of being as emerging-abiding sway, *aletheia* is the being, happening, and becoming of truth.[121]

Finally, that which emerges out of concealment will eventually recede into it once again. As Heidegger puts it,

> To be a being—this implies to be made manifest, to step forth in appearing, to set itself forth, to pro-duce something [*sich hin-stellen, etwas her-stellen*]. Not-being, in contrast, means to step away from

appearance, from presence. The essence of appearance involves this
stepping-forth and stepping-away.[122]

The dynamic, or strife, between concealment and unconcealment
recalls the notions of earth and world in "The Origin of the Work
of Art," where Heidegger states that "Earth rises up through world
and world grounds itself on the earth only insofar as truth
happens as the Ur-strife between clearing and concealment."[123]
In *Introduction to Metaphysics*, Heidegger interprets the
Heraclitean fragment, *phusis kruptesthai philei*,[124] to the same
effect:

> Being means: to appear in emerging, to step forth out of
> concealment—and for this very reason, concealment and the
> provenance from concealment essentially belong to Being. [….] Being
> remains inclined toward concealment, whether in great veiling and
> silence, or in the most superficial distorting and obscuring. The
> immediate proximity of *phusis* and *kruptesthai* reveals the intimacy of
> Being and seeming as the strife between them.[125]

The dynamic, fluctuating sway between concealment and
unconcealment also takes us back to Ibn Arabi, according to
whom every unveiling is a veiling—"The Cosmos," he maintains,
is "the veil [covering] its true self".[126]—and according to whom
"every Self-manifestation at once provides a creation and
annihilates another".[127] As in Heidegger, veiling and unveiling are
inextricably entwined in the Sufi philosopher's understanding of
unconcealment, which is unthinkable in a form unmediated by
concealment.

## Truth and Art

Tying the Heideggerian notion of truth back to the work of art,
we can clearly see that he liberates the artwork from a mimetic

understanding of truth. Instead, the work of art is a *happening* of truth in which the strife between world and earth, and their tendencies towards concealment and unconcealment, takes place. "In the work," Heidegger maintains, "the happening of truth is at work. But what is thus at work is at work *in* the work."[128] To Heidegger, then, we must seek the origin of the work in the work itself, and not in something other than itself—not in the artist or in art history, not in allegory or any other conceptual framework imposed on the artwork from outside.

The contrast with the Platonic understanding of art, where art is a copy of a copy, twice removed from truth, could not be clearer.[129] Plato's truth is self-identical, unchangeable, eternal, timeless, and real in a way that mere appearance can never be. It is ideal, not in this world, cannot be sensed, and can only be seen by the mind. Art is of no use in the quest to attain this truth. Heidegger's truth is a dynamic process that is unimaginable without appearance. It is an ontological happening that takes place in the artwork, and with which the artwork enables, as Gruber puts it for miniature art, "experiential confrontations in pictorial form."[130]

"Truth happens in Van Gogh's painting," Heidegger writes:

> That does not mean that something is correctly portrayed; it means, rather, that in the manifestation of the equipmental being of the shoe-equipment, that which is as a whole—world and earth in their counterplay—achieves unconcealment.[131]

We discover the true sense of equipment—here, the pair of peasant shoes—neither by explanation, nor by describing the pair of shoes, nor by recounting the production or actual use of the peasant shoes, "but only by bringing ourselves before Van Gogh's painting."[132] Through the painting, we see the true equipmental being of the shoes, and in manifesting this being, the work of art sets itself apart from the actual equipment itself.

Just as with the work of art, Heidegger claims that our understanding of truth is concealed under layers of preconceptions. In dismantling the oppositional preconceptions that surround the work of art—substance and accident, subject and object, matter and form—Heidegger aims to critique oppositional thinking in general, the kind of thinking that can lead us to a correspondence theory of truth in which truth is reduced to the affiliation of facts and knowledge, or to a correlation between object and concept.

Applied in science and technology, this kind of thinking posits an active human being vis-à-vis a passive or inactive world, a human (or even just a human mind) that "gives the measure and draws up the guidelines for everything that is,".[133] anointing itself a god in a godless world which it goes on to master and manipulate, ostensibly at will..[134] Heidegger's approach to the work of art, then, is rooted in his critique of the contemporary world, in which humans conceive themselves in an all-powerful and all-calculating role. The result of this oppositional approach is, as we will see below, *Unfug* or inauthentic *techne*.

## Phusis as Techne

The notion of *techne* is closely related by Heidegger to that of *dike*. Rather than its usual, reductive meaning of "justice," Heidegger takes *dike* as the manifestation of an order that is too overwhelming for human beings to grasp—such as the cosmos—but that nonetheless demonstrates a certain form of fittingness (*Fug*). Human beings may not be able to comprehend *dike*, but they can establish an authentic relation to it through the creation of works, i.e., *techne*, so that *dike* is mirrored in *techne*. On the other hand, any human work that does not do justice to *dike* is inauthentic *techne*, or *Unfug*.

Just as with *techne*, Heidegger distinguishes between authentic and inauthentic violence. All human activity, he maintains, carries a connotation of violence. Take, for example, the usage of language: inauthentic violence, here, would consist of clichés, gossip, platitudes, and the like—language paths that humans invent only to later become trapped in them, traversing them over and over again. Authentic violence, in contrast, is inflicted upon language by the poet or thinker. Here, the violence is a human need through which we clear ourselves new paths. Here lies human creativity; in the words of poet Özdemir Asaf,

> The birds are born to fly;
> We understand it from their bones being hollow.
> There is no open and known route of humans,
> We create it.[135]

Art, to Heidegger, arises out of *techne*. The artist, or *technites*, is a conduit or passageway; rather than just applying a form to matter, artists recognize a possibility of unconcealment and facilitate its occurrence. Rodin, in *The Thinker*, allows the bronze to express one of its many possibilities. Matisse maintains that his choice of colors "does not rest on any scientific theory; it is based on observation, on sensitivity, on felt experiences."[136] And Paul Klee describes the artist's role as follows:

> Standing at his appointed place, the trunk of the tree, he does nothing other than gather and pass on what comes to him from the depths. He neither serves nor rules—he transmits. His position is humble. And the beauty at the crown is not his own. He is merely a channel.[137]

The understanding of the artist as conduit ties in with the Sufi understanding of art as worship, and with the tradition whereby miniaturists would refrain from signing their works, assuming a posture of humility about their role in the creative process.[138]

Arising, as it does, out of *techne*, the work of art is an example of human violence. It is, however, an authentic form of violence, directly related to truth as unconcealment. With its strife between earth and world, and its interplay between concealment and unconcealment, the artwork shows the inability of humans to fully master the universe while at the same time transcending established ways of thinking and being human. The moment we approach the work without our preconceptions, whatever we say about it becomes strange. Words fail us, or fail to convey meaning, as Ibn Arabi relates about his own encounter with being in the mystical experience: "I saw things and I wanted to express what I saw, but could not do so, being no different from those who cannot speak."[139]

As we have seen above, Sufis regard the mystical experience as a form of "self-annihilation" in which dichotomies such as body and mind or created and creator are transcended and the Sufi abandons herself to oneness with being—a "little death" experienced during one's lifetime, albeit one from which the Sufi must return to ordinary existence and perception. Similarly, for Heidegger, death is the ultimate unknown that seduces humans towards *aletheia*.[140] Death is "an end beyond all completion," he writes, "a limit beyond all limits."[141] For this reason, death is also the originary source of all human violence, which humans inflict upon their surroundings in order to widen the extent of their mastery towards this final, unreachable limit.[142][143]

Like death, art reminds us of our own finitude. But it also gives us hope that there is no *end*—in the work of art, there will always be something that escapes our comprehension, but this also means there will always be the promise of something more. The strangeness occasioned by the work of art, then, is to be embraced. Dust Mohammad and Mustafa Ali embrace this strangeness when they describe a work of miniature art as "astonishing," "confounding," or "beyond all description." And miniature artists harness this strangeness, for instance in the Muhammad portraits that Gruber calls "purposefully destabilizing."[144]

As witnesses and conduits of unconcealment, Heidegger's human beings always participate in the creation of meaning. In this sense, being as *dike* is in need of human intermediacy for its unfolding as *techne*. This anthropocentrism is mirrored in Ibn Arabi: "It is we who make Him a divinity by being that through which He knows Himself as Divine."[145] But Heidegger also acknowledges that achieving authentic *techne* is too great a task for a limited and finite being. Ultimately, humans are bound to fail at this task—a failure also acknowledged by Ibn Arabi, who, mystical "self-annihilation" aside, insists that true unity between being and the particular can only occur in death. Still, both thinkers give a positive connotation to human failure. The most authentic course for humans is to engage the overwhelming order of being and to express this order in a kind of work, knowing full well they are doomed to fail. Such failure, so Heidegger, is the most proper *techne* of all.

## 7. The Artist as Phenomenologist:
## Merleau-Ponty and Cézanne

### Merleau-Ponty and Cézanne

In the epilogue to *The Origin of the Work of Art*, Heidegger writes that his thoughts "are concerned with the enigma of art, the enigma that art itself is. They are far from claiming to solve the enigma. The task is to see the enigma."[1] Maurice Merleau-Ponty's writings on painting could be prefaced in a similar way. In his essays "Cézanne's Doubt" (1945) and "Eye and Mind" (1961),[2] Merleau-Ponty forges his own path to painting, starting at the crossroads of Husserl and Heidegger, Frenhofer and Cézanne.

Much like Heidegger, Merleau-Ponty approaches art through a particular artist, in his case Paul Cézanne (1839–1906):

> It took him one hundred working sessions for a still life, one hundred fifty sittings for a portrait. What we call his work was, for him, only the attempt, and the approach of his painting.[3]

Thus begins "Cézanne's Doubt." The first connection between phenomenology and art lies in these carefully chosen words: Cézanne's work, to Merleau-Ponty, is not something complete, but something continually in process—or, in phenomenological terms, coming into being.

Cézanne's ceaseless "attempt" at painting is accompanied by another, equally remarkable feature: his ongoing doubt about his work. Everything in the painter's life seemed to feed into this doubt. He was disparaged by the intelligentsia of his time and even went as far as suspecting that he painted the way he did because of a visual impairment. Merleau-Ponty is fascinated by this abyss of doubt: "Why so much uncertainty, so much labor, so many failures, and, suddenly, the greatest success?"[4]

Rather than psychoanalyzing the painter, Merleau-Ponty uses Cézanne's personal life—or rather, perhaps, his ineptitude at leading a life in the midst of people—to argue for the painter's "inhuman character."[5] In Cézanne's life and work alike, Merleau-Ponty finds an "alienation of his humanity" and a retreat from the "human world" to the "visible world."[6] Cézanne, Merleau-Ponty maintains, was committed to painting "from nature"[7] and believed that even "a face should be painted as an object."[8] But what does it mean to flee the human world, become alienated from one's humanity? What is the difference between the human world and the visible world? And how does one paint "from nature"?

The key to Cézanne's work, Merleau-Ponty believes, lies neither in the painter's life nor in the artistic trends that inspired him. Rather, Cézanne's achievement was to look at nature as only a human being could who was isolated from other humans, the human world, and even his own life, unfettered by the cultural, traditional, or scientific preconceptions that humans bring to their everyday perceptions. In other words, Merleau-Ponty sees Cézanne as striving for the kind of perception that Husserl and, following him, Heidegger, would have described as a phenomenological *epoché*. Thus, Cézanne emancipated himself from art history, while his art emancipated an object hidden behind the "atmosphere" of the impressionists he so admired.[9]

## Art and Science

How does Merleau-Ponty view Cézanne's perception of the world, and the process by which he transforms this perception into art? "Fleshly eyes," the philosopher writes, "are already much more than receptors for beams of light, color, lines."[10] Eyes are "gifted" with vision—rather than mere tools for seeing, they are "computers of the world."[11]

But in order to earn such a gift, one needs practice. To come into full possession of vision, the painter must train her eyes, as did Cézanne, who visited the Louvre every day while in Paris.[12] Further, the artist studied geometry, anatomy, and geology to acquire the education he felt he needed in science as well as art. As Merleau-Ponty puts it, the effort of painting "may require the creation of new materials or new means of expression, but it may well be realized at times by the reexamination and reuse of those already at hand".[13]—a point of which, as we have seen, Henri Matisse was well aware: "one gives oneself all the more readily when one sees one's efforts confirmed by a tradition.".[14]

Knowledge of science, tradition, and technique, however, can only be the first step. The artist, so Merleau-Ponty, needs to distinguish between "the human order of ideas and sciences" and "the spontaneous order of perceived things".[15] Cézanne's real aspiration, Merleau-Ponty claims, is to confront the sciences with this "spontaneous order" from which they emanated, "put[ting] intelligence, ideas, sciences, perspective and tradition back in touch with the world of nature which they were intended to comprehend.".[16]

At the outset of "Eye and Mind," Merleau-Ponty echoes Heidegger's critique of scientific investigation: "Science manipulates things and gives up dwelling in them.".[17] After its historical divorce from philosophy, Merleau-Ponty claims, science loses touch with the primordial world and starts confronting it from a distance. In the words of Hugh Silverman,

> Scientific thought does not want to enter into the visible. It wants to stand back from the visible in order to provide rules, regularities, and models for understanding it.[18]

Merleau-Ponty opposes this attitude to what he calls "classical science," which apprehends the "opaqueness" of the world and tries to embrace this opaqueness rather than retreat from it..[19] This "bold way of thinking".[20] is abandoned by science once it begins positing every being as an object for itself, thereby distancing itself from its own ostensible goal of unconcealing the world.

Taking his cues from Husserl and Heidegger, Merleau-Ponty sees the scientist as dwelling in a pre-given notion of humanity instead of reaching out to primordial existence. Rather than a peasant immersing in the earth to let it bring forth new fruit, he is either a scavenger, picking up whatever he finds, or an exploiter, forcing the earth to reshape according to his expectations rather than reveal its own potential. This antagonistic relationship between humans and their environment is succinctly expressed in Sophocles' *Antigone*, which Heidegger quotes at length in *Introduction to Metaphysics*:

He moves across the white-capped ocean seas
blasted by winter storms, carving his way
under the surging waves engulfing him.
With his teams of horses he wears down
the unwearied and immortal earth,
the oldest of the gods, harassing her,
as year by year his ploughs move back and forth..[21]

Having thus become "autonomous," Merleau-Ponty claims, science comes to regard its function as transforming and exploiting the world rather than grasping it..[22] "Thinking 'operationally' becomes a sort of absolute artificialism,".[23] he writes, suggesting an idea of "operationalism" that Marjorie Grene further explains as "the belief that all problems can be solved by the experimental manipulation of precisely specified variables.".[24] This conception of science, transforming both humans and their environment into "manipulanda," is bound to lead humanity into a "nightmare".[25] without the possibility of awakening.

What science lacks is an understanding of itself. The thought of science, Merleau-Ponty maintains, should be "placed back in the 'there is' which precedes it.".[26] Science needs to acknowledge and reconnect with its base, a base that Merleau-Ponty calls the "brute or existent" world and describes, echoing the Heideggerian strife between earth and world, as "the soil of the sensible world and the soil of the worked-upon world.".[27]

Merleau-Ponty also follows Heidegger's lead in claiming that we are so accustomed to the operationalist attitude and the artificial objects it creates that we often merely perceive these objects via the human actions which put them to use, entertaining no doubt as to their necessity or reliability. Cézanne's paintings, so Merleau-Ponty, shake our world in such a way that we are no longer able to lose ourselves within the safe borders of such habitual thoughts and are thrown at the doors of an inhuman, primordial nature. "Once art is present," Merleau-Ponty maintains, "it awakens powers that are asleep in ordinary vision, a secret preexistence.".[28] To the philosopher, "Art, and especially painting draw from this pool of brute sense, about which activism wants to know nothing. Art and painting alone do this in full innocence.".[29]

## Painting and Writing

Merleau-Ponty contrasts the potential of art to that of writing. "From the writer and the philosopher," he says, "we want opinions and advice. We will not allow them to hold the world suspended.".[30] What Merleau-Ponty envisions is a suspension of "humanity"—all the universals accepted as such, all so-called "stable truths" upon which we construct new "truths," including even the very sentences we form—enabling a return, a homecoming to the primordial, to that which is prior to "humanity" or human-made values. The painter is privileged in his ability to perform such a suspension and let the primordial existence show itself without a veil. As Merleau-Ponty puts it, "Only the painter is entitled to gaze upon everything without being obliged to appraise what he sees."[31]

Nonetheless, Merleau-Ponty also finds a parallel between painting and writing. Just as "a picture is not a trompe l'œil," he writes, "words do not *resemble* what they designate."[32] As a matter of fact, painting and phenomenological writing can serve the same purpose: Cézanne expresses in painting what phenomenology endeavors to articulate indirectly via philosophical language, namely pre-reflexive perception.[33] As Husserl's phenomenological method aims to emancipate itself from the presuppositions of the Galilean and Cartesian traditions, Merleau-Ponty believed that Cézanne—and he himself—faced the same dilemma: a new way is needed, a way to emancipate oneself from dichotomous ways of thinking and overcome the split between self and world, subject and object.

While Merleau-Ponty sees Cézanne's paintings as a prime example of phenomenological work through painting, the question remains open to what extent writing itself can serve as a locus of the phenomenological *epoché*, or the self-manifestation of the absolute. On the one hand, I argued above that the Sufi tradition regards words as too closely tied to rational meaning to serve as effective vehicles for apprehending the absolute. On the other hand, though, it is clear that writers such as Ibn Arabi and Merleau-Ponty are stylistically and structurally concerned with ensuring their texts go beyond conveying "opinions and advice" and have the potential to "purposefully destabilize" their readers.

## Vision and Synesthesia

Cézanne, Merleau-Ponty asserts, always seeks for his "motif," which is nothing less than "the landscape in its totality and in its absolute fullness."[34] The terms "totality" and "absolute fullness" seem to suggest a monolithic state, but nothing could be further from what Merleau-Ponty has in mind. Rather, the painter strives "to unveil (*dévoiler*) the means, which are nothing but visible, by which the mountain makes itself into a mountain before our eyes."[35]

The mountain, then, is not a mountain in any stable, unchanging sense: it is engaged in a continuous process of becoming or coming-into-being. In Jean-François Lyotard's words, "Cézanne desired [...] Mount Sainte-Victoire to cease being a visual object and become an event in the visual field."[36] And according to Mikel Dufrenne, "Cézanne does not reconstruct, he pre-constructs. He does not shatter the fruit bowl, he shows us its genesis, that is, not its production but its coming into the visible."[37] Cézanne's goal is to depict things in both their stability and their instability; his intention is to paint "matter as it takes on form."[38]

For a painter pursuing this unstable process of coming-into-being, there can be "only one lyricism," Merleau-Ponty maintains: that of "the continual rebirth of existence."[39] As Françoise Dastur puts it, this approach challenges "every question of origin [and] every evolutionary perspective,"[40] regarding the process of becoming as "one sole explosion of Being which is forever."[41] The parallels to Ibn Arabi's "Breath of the Merciful" are clear. To the Sufi also, the process of creation is inherently unstable, "constitutes an imbalance in Nature,"[42] and is constantly recurring, with each instant producing and destroying the cosmos as a unique manifestation of the absolute.[43]

To apprehend this coming-into-being, we must emancipate ourselves from all judgments which continually prearrange appearances according to a pre-formed order, not just on a conceptual, but also on a perceptual level. The goal is what Dufrenne describes as "the Husserlian model of passive synthesis":

> This vision does not organize the visible, nor does it bestow a meaning upon it or constitute it as readable and expressible in words. It receives the visible, rising from an invisible that still clings to it; one can say at the very most that vision opens itself to the visible which is given to it.[44]

Even the distinction between the senses, to Merleau-Ponty, is a preconception that may cloud our brute perception, in which "we *see* the depth, the smoothness, softness, the hardness of objects; Cézanne even claimed that we see the odor.".[45] This is synesthesia, i.e., an overlap and blending of different sense perceptions. Perhaps, the painter sees the smell of the coffee I am drinking right now; perhaps the coffee tastes like a color; is the sound of the forks on the table a shade of yellow? "Cézanne," Merleau-Ponty writes, "would be handing himself over to the chaos of the sensations.".[46] Indeed, it is a "world almost mad," "a delirium which is vision.".[47]

## The Task of Translation

The painter's task is to translate the delirium of synesthesia back into the purely visible form of painting. This is a paradoxical task: on the one hand, it means "aiming for reality while denying himself the means to attain it," which Merleau-Ponty, paraphrasing Emile Bernard, calls a form of suicide.[48] On the other hand, it means a return to "humanity" and an employment of its means: "What was at issue, all science forgotten, was to capture, *through* these sciences, the constitution of the landscape as an emerging organism."[49]

This is where technique comes into play. Perhaps the most important tool in Cézanne's technical arsenal is color. "The dimension of colour," Merleau-Ponty writes, "creates—from itself to itself—identities, differences, a texture, a materiality, a something."[50] Cézanne's synesthetic usage of color has not escaped scholarly attention. As Simona Erjavec puts it, Cézanne believed that "a certain thing would not possess a certain color if it didn't possess a certain shape, tactile given, sonority, smell."[51] The goal in painting, then, is to achieve the kind of color that will, at the same time, manifest all other attributes of the thing as well.

Cézanne also uses color to undermine a conventional apprehension of space. In the painter's later watercolors, "space [...] radiates around planes that cannot be assigned to any place at all." Merleau-Ponty talks of "a superimposing of transparent surfaces" and "a flowing movement of places of colour which overlap, advance and retreat."[52] But while Cézanne's color work unfetters the object, it still keeps its relations to its surroundings intact; the object is not lost in these relations.[53]

The artist achieves these effects by meticulously covering the canvas with tiny strokes of color, similar to the pointillist technique (or the composition of a digital image out of distinct pixels). When the painting is approached, each stroke of color is recognized as a separate and complete unit in itself. In contrast, when one retreats from the painting, the interaction of these strokes leads one to perceive larger, homogenous blocks of color and shape. Thus, the image literally emerges from a chaos of perception as the viewer interacts with the painting.

Turning from color to perspective, Merleau-Ponty notes that to Cézanne, our actual perception has little to do with geometric or photographic perspective—an insight with which miniature painters would have surely agreed. "The perspective of the Renaissance," Merleau-Ponty writes, "is no infallible 'gimmick.'"[54] Rather, as Dastur puts it, it is "a cultural fact, a moment of painting that makes the mistake of setting itself up as an infallible technique and a fundamental law."[55]

Cézanne's pursuit of lived over geometric perspective leads him to combine a number of perspectives from which the objects in the painting might be approached. In so doing, Cézanne succeeds in "shattering the viewer's expectations of a space that would operate according to Cartesian principles"[56] and enables the objects to gradually reveal themselves as they may to a person circling around them and regarding them from a variety of vantage points:

> It is Cézanne's genius that when the overall composition of the picture is seen globally, perspectival distortions are no longer visible in their own right but rather contribute, as they do in natural vision, to the impression of an emerging order, an object in the act of appearing, organizing itself before our eyes.[57]

By the same token, Cézanne rejects the traditional usage of contour. The contour of an object, considered as a line enclosing the object, is more relevant to geometry than the visible world, where there are no outlines. As John Sallis puts it,

> One sees the line and yet does not see it. One sees the contour of the apple and yet sees nothing other than the apple contoured against the background. One sees the border between the field and the meadow, and yet whatever one sees is either field or meadow, not the border.[58]

For this reason, Cézannian outline is an effect of colors rather than a single line, making the distinction between color and contour disappear. Like with Cézanne's other techniques, this allows the painting to manifest an order of things in the process of emerging rather than perfected and immutable: "To outline just one single contour," Merleau-Ponty writes, "sacrifices depth—that is, the dimension which gives us the thing, not as spread out before us, but as full of reserves and as an inexhaustible reality".[59]

As we can see, Cézanne's approach has little to do with "realism" or "verisimilitude" as typically understood by art criticism. This does not mean, however, that he rejects the idea of a painting that is faithful to the experience of perception—he simply does not find so-called verisimilitude particularly faithful in this sense. This objection to verisimilitude highlights the limits of an art criticism that proceeds from the a priori assumption of a single and universal standard of "realism" and labels everything as "abstract" that deviates from this standard—as we encountered in Western scholarly approaches to miniature painting above. As Merleau-Ponty puts it,

> A figure flattened down onto a plane surface scarcely retains the forms of things; it is a deformed figure that must be deformed—the square becomes a lozenge, the circle an oval—in order to present the object. It is an image of the object only on the condition of "not resembling it."[60]

## The Homecoming of the Artist

We have seen that Cézanne's artistic mission, as described by Merleau-Ponty, demands an estrangement from conventional ways of thinking and perceiving—an "ecstatic process,"[61] in Rachel McCann's words, that enables the painter's extraordinary vision. Subsequently, however, the painter must overcome this *ekstasis* to translate her vision back into a (visual) language comprehensible to the viewers of her art.

Such a state of "homelessness" is also discussed by Heidegger, followed by a "homecoming" in which humans are able to open themselves to others while also preserving their self-identity, namely *Dasein*. *Da*, the German word for "there," is where humans "ek-sist" in a state of "nearness to Being." The Sufi, finally, faces a similar task. She must depart from the familiar world in order to attain her mystical insight, followed by her return to the familiar and her attempt at conveying her insight in comprehensible terms.

The artist, philosopher, or Sufi is not a divine creator. Nonetheless, she has to create out of *nothing*, express something that has not yet found expression or meaning in human terms, but that will come to bear a meaning as soon as it is revealed through her work. Even she herself does not know the meaning of what she expresses: hers is a cry beckoning a meaning. "The artist," Merleau-Ponty writes, "launches his work just as a human once launched the first word, not knowing whether it will be anything more than a shout.".[62]

> The painter can do no more than construct an image. It is necessary to wait for this image to come to life for others. Then, the work of art will have joined together these separate lives; it will no longer exist in only one of them like a stubborn dream or a persistent delirium, nor will it exist in a space as a colored piece of canvas. It will dwell undivided in several minds, presumably in every possible mind, as an acquisition for always..[63]

The outcome envisioned by Merleau-Ponty—the artwork finding a place, comprehension, and recognition in culture, perhaps even serving as a unifying force in the culture or the world at large—harkens back to Qadi Ahmad's eulogy to the famed Ibrahim Mirza album:

> Youths represented with sunlike faces, in shame,
> Had closed their lips in their conversation.

> All of them united in war and peace,
> Not like the dwellers of the world full of hypocrisy and dishonor!
> Day and night companions of the same quarters,
> Men devoid of discord in their communion![64]

The description, of course, refers to the figures in the album, contrasting their harmony on paper with the discord found in the world. Nonetheless, it also reads as an exhortation to the world to follow the example of art.

It is more likely, however, that the work resulting from the "homecoming"—a homecoming Heidegger claims has been absent from Western thought since the Pre-Socratics[65]—will be met with incomprehension, rejection, or even condemnation. Cézanne's doubt, fuelled by the often-negative reception of his work during his lifetime, is a mild version of this phenomenon, as is Ibn Arabi's assertion that "I saw things and I wanted to express what I saw, but could not do so, being no different from those who cannot speak."[66] Perhaps, just like Cézanne, Ibn Arabi doubted his very ability to ever convey his perceptions. More extreme versions are Sheikh San'an, whose disciples are bewildered by his outrageous displays of love for the Christian princess, such as herding swine and destroying a copy of the Quran, and al-Hallaj, who faced torture and execution for his ostensible claim to divinity.

Perhaps the work of art cannot help but elicit a negative response—it is, after all, "purposefully destabilizing." Cézanne's world, too, is destabilizing; it inhibits all human ease. "Cézanne's people are strange," so Merleau-Ponty, "as if viewed by a creature of another species."[67] After Cézanne, he claims, the work of other painters makes the viewer feel back at home.[68] But this kind of reassuring pleasure belongs to culture rather than art. When creating culture, we merely re-create what we are already acquainted with, and when exposed to culture, we are on familiar ground. True painting, however, is not tied to civilization, nation, belief, or reason, but rather tries to overcome such givens. "Figurative or not," Merleau-Ponty writes, "painting celebrates no other enigma but that of visibility."_[69]

What happens, though, once a work of art becomes appropriated and assimilated by culture? Does it lose its disruptive and transformative potential? Not according to Merleau-Ponty, who believes that the "message" of a true work of art cannot be fixed by the beholder. Just as Frenhofer's masterpiece motivated its viewers to move, advance, and retreat in search of the best vantage point to regard it, we do not so much look "at" a painting as we see "according to it."_[70] In Husserlian terms, Merleau-Ponty asserts that there is always an excess in the work of art and a lack in the perceiver. Exemplary paintings always hold a promise of further meanings, yet to be discovered:

> As for the history of works of art, in any case, if they are great, the sense we give to them after the fact has issued from them. It is the work itself that has opened the field from which it appears in another light. It metamorphoses *itself* and *becomes* what follows; the interminable reinterpretations to which it is *legitimately* susceptible change it only into itself. And if the historian unearths beneath its manifest content a surplus and thickness of sense, the texture which was preparing a long future, then this active manner of being, this possibility he unveils in the work, this monograph he finds there—all are grounds for a philosophical meditation._[71]

## Man Added to Nature

As we have seen, the Merleau-Pontian artist cannot take conscious charge of the process of artistic expression or creation._[72] "The artist cannot intend," Günter Figal argues, "the painter's will must come to silence. All voices of prejudice have to become tacit;

the painter has to forget, to be silent in order to be nothing but an echo.".[73] As Merleau-Ponty puts it,

> Art is not skillful construction, skillful artifice, the skillful relation, from the outside, to a space and a world. It is truly the "inarticulate cry," as Hermes Trismegistus said, "which seemed to be the voice of the light.".[74]

Just like Heidegger, to whom the artist is a conduit, Merleau-Ponty views the artist not as a creator but an intermediary. "In a poem," Merleau-Ponty paraphrases Apollinaire, "there are phrases which do not appear to have been *created*, which seem to have *formed themselves*.".[75] The world, in this view, is acting *through* the artist, including her technical means, rather than bending to her will. In Taylor Carman's words,

> It is not surprising that painters sometimes say they feel as if things are looking at them. The idea of inspiration, too, implies being invaded and inhabited by the world, as opposed to acting on it. This sense of bodily communion with the world is crucial to the art of painting..[76]

While this role of conduit points to a certain passivity, the artist cannot be reduced to this passive role; after all, it is only her own, subjective contribution that can elevate art beyond a mere imitation of nature—as Mustafa Ali puts it, it is only the artist who can "give a visible form" to things that are "impossible to represent as matter.".[77] Our Middle Eastern sources do not elaborate further on the process by which the artist may accomplish this task. But turning to Merleau-Ponty, we gain an appreciation of how the artist's unique contribution takes place.

"Cézanne," Merleau-Ponty writes, "was able to revive the classical definition of art: man added to nature.".[78] He quotes the artist himself: "The landscape thinks itself in me, and I am its consciousness.".[79] This is where Merleau-Ponty makes his move against a mimetic understanding of art. If Cézanne is the consciousness of landscape, he is not its imitator but its spokesperson; rather than copying it, he lends it a voice. Without the painter, we cannot hear the voice of the landscape. He makes the inaudible audible, the invisible visible—in short, he allows that which has not yet become manifest to manifest itself.

The painter becoming the consciousness of the landscape, and lending a voice to it, mirrors Balzac's description of Frenhofer, who becomes "art incarnate," thereby expressing "its mysteries, its vehement passion and its dreams,".[80] as well as Heidegger's thoughts on Van Gogh's painting, which enables the philosopher to meditate on the equipmentality of the equipment, letting a world unconceal itself via the peasant shoes.

## The Imaginary

How does a painter become the consciousness, the voice of the landscape? Merleau-Ponty quotes Cézanne: "Nature is on the inside.".[81] By positing that nature is not simply something in front of the painter and observed by him, but rather something within him, Cézanne subverts any dichotomous understanding of human and nature, painter and landscape, or inside and outside; he speaks of wanting to "unite" nature and art..[82] Merleau-Ponty understands this goal not as some kind of simplistic, undifferentiated unity, but rather a complex interweaving:

> Quality, light, color, depth, which are over there before us, are there only because they awaken an echo in our bodies and because the body welcomes them. Why would this internal equivalence, this carnal formula of their presence that the things arouse in me, not arouse an outline that is again visible, in which every other gaze would find again the motifs that support their inspection of the world?.[83]

The painter cultivates an awareness of what Merleau-Ponty calls "dimensions"—the factors that enable visual perception while remaining invisible themselves. Through these factors, such as light, color, and depth, visible things arouse an invisible equivalent of themselves within the perceiver: "Rather than seeing it," Merleau-Ponty writes, "I see according to, or with it".[84] It follows that the invisible equivalent is not "a tracing, copy, second thing"[85] that merely imitates the visible thing, but complements and completes the visible thing in an indispensable way:

> Neither the drawing nor the picture belongs to the in-itself any more than the image does. They are the inside of the outside and the outside of the inside, which duplicity of sensing makes possible and without which we would never understand the quasi-presence and imminent visibility which make up the whole problem of the imaginary.[86]

This "imaginary" is crucial to Merleau-Ponty's thought. It fulfills a unique function far beyond replicating an actual thing: "The imaginary is much nearer to and much farther away from the actual." It is "much nearer" because it creates an equivalent of the actual inside the perceiver. And it is much farther away since it offers the perceiver something the actual cannot: what Merleau-Ponty calls the "traces of the vision of the inside," or "the imaginary texture of the real".[87]

Thanks to the imaginary, the painter perceives the actual thing in its visibility and its invisibility. She is aware of the objects of ordinary vision as well as the invisible factors that condition vision itself—such as light and depth. This perception, in turn, leads to a painting in which, as Trevor Perri puts it, "presence and absence, reality and unreality, and visibility and invisibility inherently participate with or are implied in one another".[88] In a way, then, Merleau-Ponty sees the painting as more real than the actual thing—or, to put it in the Husserlian terminology of lack:

> The eye sees the world, and it sees what the world lacks in order to be a painting, and what the picture lacks in order to be itself, and, on the palette, the colours for which the picture is waiting; and it sees, once it is done, the picture that responds to all these lacks, and it sees the paintings of others, the other responses to all these lacks..[89]

### Absolute Vision

Clearly, when a human being gazes upon something, she wants to see more than what meets the eye. This points to the privileged role Merleau-Ponty ascribes to human beings as "perceivers" of the world. Not solely concerned with survival like the other animal species, humans are something more: they are seekers of truth. "Animals," Merleau-Ponty opines, "cannot *gaze at* things, cannot penetrate them in expectation of nothing but the truth.".[90]

However, Merleau-Ponty does not reduce the uniqueness of human perception to humans' mental agency; rather, he insists that human perception can only result from the unity of body and mind. His "vision" is a carnal kind of perception, not judging the world from the outside, but "digesting" it on the inside:

> There is no vision without thought, but it is not enough to think in order to see. Vision is a conditioned thought; it is born "as occasioned" by what happens in the body; it is "incited" to think by the body. It does not choose either to be or not to be or to think this thing or that..[91]

These ideas run parallel to those of Ibn Arabi, for whom, as we have seen, only human beings can achieve a total perception of the absolute—a perception from which animals are barred for mental reasons and angels for bodily ones. To Ibn Arabi, all perception is localized and enabled through the body: A thing "appears to itself in a form that is invested by the location of the vision by that which would only appear to it given the existence of the location."[92] In the case of the painter, so Merleau-Ponty, the body then goes on to complete the circle by giving back to the world: "We cannot see how a Mind could paint. It is by lending his body to the world that the artist changes the world into painting."[93]

But how can the body both trap the perceiver in a limited vantage point and at the same time enable a perception of the absolute? Once again, let us turn to Merleau-Ponty in search of an answer. "The world," Merleau-Ponty writes, "is made of the very stuff of the body," which is "caught in the fabric of the world."[94] Body, world, and perception, then, are all made of the same fabric, or, as Merleau-Ponty puts it, the same "flesh." This "flesh," to Merleau-Ponty, is "brute and wild being,"[95] the unconscious ground of conscious experience, an ontological basis or a condition of possibility as such. It precedes the dichotomy between self and other as well as any identification of individual beings. In "the experience of flesh," Dastur writes, "perceiving and perceived are still undivided," and "things are experienced as annexes or extensions of ourselves."[96]

A certain body can perceive things, but it is also visible to the things it perceives—and to itself as a thing among them. The perceiver, so Merleau-Ponty, "sees himself seeing; he touches himself touching; he is visible and sensitive for himself."[97] If the body could not see itself or touch itself, sense itself, experience itself, it would not be able to see or sense the things around it either. "The self loses all of its Cartesian isolation," as McCann puts it, "and exists as a self only through its intertwining as perceiver with the perceived."[98] As Merleau-Ponty's concept of "flesh" suggests, the body is inextricably embedded in this network before there is any kind of perceiving subject.

This embeddedness leads Merleau-Ponty to speak of a "fundamental narcissism of all vision,"[99] in which "the seer and the visible reciprocate one another and we no longer know which sees and which is seen."[100] This vision is "narcissistic" because whatever I see, and whatever I am seen by, is ultimately made up of the same stuff. It is universal and "anonymous"[101] because, in the endless interplay of perceiver and perceived, it resists any kind of subjectivity. All in all, it is "a total or absolute vision, outside of which nothing remains, and which closes itself back up upon" both perceiver and perceived.[102] In the theological parlance of Ibn Arabi, "there would appear to be observer and observed," while in reality, "only He sees Himself alone through Himself."[103]

Like Ibn Arabi, Merleau-Ponty turns to the mirror—both as thing and as metaphor—to illustrate his idea of absolute vision.[104] "The mirror emerges because I am both seeing and visible," he writes, "because there is a reflexivity of the sensible; the mirror translates and reproduces that reflexivity. Through it, my outside becomes complete."[105] A Sufi might phrase her own views in similar terms: "The particulars, and especially humans," she might say, "are both seeing and visible, acting as mirrors through which the absolute becomes visible to itself. Through their reflection, the absolute becomes complete." The following passage from Merleau-Ponty once again illustrates how fruitful it can be to read certain phenomenological texts as non-theological companion pieces to Sufi thought:

> The mirror's phantom draws my flesh outside, and at the same time the invisible of my body can invest the other bodies that I see. Hence, my body can include segments drawn from the body of others. Just as my substance passes into them; man is a mirror for man. Mirrors are instruments of a universal magic that changes things into spectacles and spectacles into things, me into another and another into me.[106]

## Cartesian Vision

The significance of the mirror in Merleau-Ponty and Ibn Arabi alike could not stand in starker contrast to the "Cartesian model of vision," which, so Merleau-Ponty, "is modeled after the sense of touch".[107] Here, if there is nothing to touch—as with a reflection in a mirror—there really is nothing to see, either: "The blind," Descartes writes, "see with their hands".[108] For the Cartesian, a reflection is only a deceiver; he

> does not see himself in the mirror; he sees a puppet, an "outside," which, he has every reason to believe, other people see in the very same way, but which is no more for himself than for others a flesh. His "image" in the mirror is an effect of the mechanics of things. If he recognizes himself in it, if he thinks it "looks like him," it is thought that weaves this connection. The specular image is in no sense a part of him.[109]

Merleau-Ponty extends his criticism of Descartes to the latter's views on painting as expressed in his *Optics*. "When [Descartes] speaks of 'pictures' [tableaux]," Merleau-Ponty writes, "he takes drawing as typical." This is because drawings "preserve the form of objects":[110]

> They present the object by its outside, or its envelopment. If he had examined that other, deeper opening upon things given us by the secondary qualities, especially color, then—since there is no rule governed or projective relationship between them and the true properties of things, and we understand their message all the same— he would have found himself faced with the problem of a conceptless universality and opening upon things.[111]

Merleau-Ponty views Descartes' reduction of painting to drawing as typical of his tendency to dismiss the true complexity of the world in favor of an artificial clarity. Rather than "haunt the visible," Descartes would "reconstruct it according to the model of the visible that [...] thought has provided for itself."[112] Teasingly, Merleau-Ponty echoes the Cartesian longing for clarity and consistency: "How crystal clear everything would be in our philosophy if only we would exorcise these spectres, make illusions or objectless perceptions out of them, brush them to one side of an unequivocal world!"[113]

The philosophical ideal pursued by Descartes ultimately derives from Plato's famous line which, as we discussed earlier, divides a higher realm of forms, ideas, and mathematical truths from a lower realm of objects and appearances. It is this same line that divides the philosophical approaches of rationalism and empiricism—as well as the fields of philosophy, science, and art, dismissing art as a mere copy or imitation, secondary to appearances that are already secondary to thoughts, ideas, and forms.

From Merleau-Ponty's perspective, Plato's line appears as an icon of a metaphysics that reaches its zenith with Descartes and its nadir with Nietzsche, an icon that must be destroyed to enable a new metaphysics avoiding the dualism of the Cartesian worldview. From a Sufi perspective, in turn, it is Plato's line, rather than any figural form of representation, that appears as the true icon that the seeker of truth needs to destroy if she hopes to "seal" the division between the manifest and the unmanifest. It is this shared quest of demolishing Plato's line that renders both approaches truly "iconoclastic."

### Imperfect Interweaving

While Merleau-Ponty seems focused on abolishing dichotomies such as subject-object or matter-form, his ultimate aim is to crack the duality between noumena and phenomena, i.e., primordial existence and humanity. To Merleau-Ponty, there is no "pure invisibility," no thing-in-itself lurking in the background. Being does not have an "invisible existence" besides its visible one; it simply conceals itself in order to unconceal itself, "dissimulates itself in order to show the thing." The visible, not the invisible, is the ground; if there is no visible, there is no thing either. As Johnson puts it,

> The lines of visible things are doubled by a lining of invisibility, and this in-visible lining is in the visible. Merleau-Ponty stresses this, and by doing so de-centers the ordinary religious or aesthetic search away from the pursuit of an invisibility that would be a separate reality, a heavenly world apart from this world. [....] Paradoxical as it may sound, therefore, Merleau-Ponty's spirituality is quite consistent with a certain qualified atheism..[114]

As I have argued above, Ibn Arabi also offers the possibility of viewing the manifestations—or the visible—as the ground for the invisible. Describing the process of creation in terms of a triplicity, the Sufi philosopher stresses the interdependence of all components of the triplicity, such as creator, creation, and creative act; or lover, beloved, and love. There is no creator without a creation. It is this reversibility between the manifest and unmanifest, or noumena and phenomena, that makes it impossible for Ibn Arabi to maintain the superiority of one to the other or, as a matter of fact, any kind of duality.

Despite this reversibility, neither Merleau-Ponty nor Ibn Arabi believes that a perfect mirroring between perceiver and perceived, subject and object, or manifestation and the absolute, is attainable. To Merleau-Ponty, things are never fully familiar to us even though we are made up of the same flesh. There is no exact coincidence between me as perceiver and perceived, or me as perceiver and the thing that is perceived. Rather than completely overlapping, perceiver and perceived are complexly interwoven. "In the mirror," as Johnson puts it, "the reflection of the right hand is transposed as the left hand. There is asymmetrical reversibility, reflexivity with difference."[115]

Sufism addresses this imperfect interweaving via the metaphor of the veil. To Ibn Arabi, the manifestations of the absolute are veils for the absolute as unmanifest. However, as we have already discussed, these veils should not be thought of as obstacles that prevent us from seeing the reality. Rather, they function somewhat like the "mask" in Friedrich Nietzsche's *The Birth of Tragedy*, where art acts as a mask that shows us the truth while protecting us from being destroyed—like Oedipus—by its overwhelming potency. We do not see the absolute despite the manifestations, Ibn Arabi maintains, but through them. In Merleau-Ponty's words,

> When through the water's thickness I see the tiled bottom of the pool, I do not see it despite the water and the reflections; I see it through them and because of them. If there were no distortions, no ripples of sunlight, if I saw, without this flesh, the geometry of the tiles, then I would stop seeing the tiled bottom as it is, where it is.[116]

Finally, Merleau-Ponty uses the concept of *écart* (gap).[117] to demonstrate the process of imperfect interweaving. The body touches (perceives), and is touched (perceived) at the same time— and yet, it must shift between the two actions or positions, resulting in an *écart* between the two. The uncertainty whether one is touching or being touched, and the reversibility of the two actions, makes it impossible to speak of them in neatly dualistic terms.

When the inner is the outer and the outer is the inner, what belongs to me and what to the world? This is the kind of uncertainty that both Merleau-Ponty and Ibn Arabi would like to provoke since it has the potential to wake us from our preconceptions and reconnect us with "others who haunt me and whom I haunt; 'others' along with whom I haunt a single, present, and actual Being as no animal has ever haunted the others of his species, territory, or habitat."[118]

# Conclusion:
# Towards a Phenomenology of Miniature Painting

## *The Illuminated Manuscript as a Great Work of Art*

The dismemberment of illuminated manuscripts at the hands of Western collectors and vendors led to a tragic loss of meaning, the kind of meaning that could only be conveyed by the entirety of the manuscript and that perished in isolated contemplation of the single miniature painting. "Only those illustrated Persian volumes," Michael Barry writes, "that have survived intact the twentieth century's depredations now allow reconstruction of what such pictures were really supposed to mean."[1]

This "meaning" of the miniature painting, so Barry, lies in "the allegorical code underlying its designs."[2] In other words, if we were to peruse an undamaged manuscript and familiarize ourselves with the text it contained—epic tales, Sufi allegories, and the like—this text would provide us with the key to unlock the paintings' code, with the result that we could read them like the text itself.

Doubtlessly, this is true. But I would like to go further—I believe that artistically, there is much more at stake in the illuminated manuscript than the mutual reinforcement of writing and painting. Rather, I think we can view the manuscript in its entirety as a great work of art in the Heideggerian sense, one that simultaneously serves to "set forth the earth"[3] and "set up a world,"[4] as in the example of the Greek temple.

"To set forth the earth," Heidegger writes, "means to bring it into the open as the self-secluding."[5] As a relatively small, portable object, the manuscript does not have the temple's constant relationship with the surrounding ground, air, light, and darkness. But the materiality of the manuscript, with its components such as paper, leather, pigments, and ink, gathers the earthly aspect of the Sufi's world in all its geographical breadth while also processing these components in such a way that their raw form remains "secluded."

When it comes to setting up a world, Sinclair reminds us that art does not simply express a culture, but "achieves, establishes and opens this culture itself."[6] This is precisely what is done by the illuminated manuscript. Without it, the interregional networks—of production, trade, curation, and so on—that are required to gather the manuscript's material components would not come into being. In other words, the creation of an illuminated manuscript does not only make a world reveal itself, it actually brings a world into being.

The manuscript does not only gather its viewers—a decidedly small number—but also the various people who serve in its creation. These people, from the gatherer of color pigments in India to the paper maker in Egypt and the bookbinder in Persia, will never meet in person but come together in the manuscript. We are far removed here from the modern cliché of the artist as solitary genius or originator of the artwork. Instead, each participant in the creation of the manuscript emerges as a conduit for the work's self-disclosure—as in the Heideggerian notion of *techne*, in which the artist (*technites*) takes on the role of a conduit facilitating the event of unconcealment.

The setting up of a world as performed by the illuminated manuscript goes beyond the gathering of *technites* who serve as conduits—it also involves the gathering of the various fields of endeavor that make up the Sufi's world. Areas of expertise as disparate and seemingly unconnected as philosophy, literature, calligraphy, painting, and leatherwork come together in the manuscript to reveal the complementarity that makes them into constituent parts of their world, and, in this gathering, perform a setting up of that world.

In the illuminated manuscript, earth and world do not confront each other as two independent, opposing powers, but commingle in the interlaced, interdependent way that Heidegger describes as strife. Take the example of color: if we think of colors as mere materiality, an earthly aspect of the miniature painting, we ignore all that the production and utilization of these colors tells us about the painting's world. It is only when aided by earth, then, that world can reveal itself in any specific way. And the same holds in reverse: through its world, each color manifests itself in a culturally charged way, acquiring a particularity that it does not reveal on its own.

Finally, Heidegger's temple also helps us transcend the representational aspect of the miniature painting. The statue inside the temple "is not a portrait intended to make it easier to recognize what the god looks like. It is, rather, a work which allows the god himself to presence and *is*, therefore, the god himself."[7] One could not ask for a more perfect parallel to the "life-giving" quality ascribed to painting by Qadi Ahmad—a quality connected not to verisimilitude, but to the self-manifestation of the absolute as occasioned by the painting. In Ibn Arabi's words, we could say that the miniature painting is "the Self-manifestation of God to the consciousness of the worshiper in this particular mode of manifestation."[8]

As Heidegger reminds us, worlds—and works—have a historicity. The fragility of a world is expressed in the destruction of its works—one need only remember the example of Gauhar Sultan, who responded to the murder of her husband, the prince Ibrahim Mirza, by washing out the priceless miniature album commissioned by the ruler. This tragic act of destruction takes on added poignancy when the water dissolving the album is read as a metaphor for time and its corrosion of the court milieu that Ibrahim Mirza had built.

The end of the artwork is more than a mere metaphor for the end of Ibrahim Mirza's rule. Rather, the artwork only ceases to be when its world does as well—as long as Ibrahim Mirza's court was intact, it would have been inconceivable to destroy the album. But the moment its world ceases to be, the work of art also loses something: the component that makes it "great," that enables it to act as the key to this particular world. The epoch has ended not because the manuscripts are destroyed, but precisely because they now *can* be destroyed.

By the time the Western art industry took it upon itself to dismember specific illuminated manuscripts, the world in which those artworks belonged had already disappeared. The same holds for the Greek temple: if the Athenians still believed in the gods of the acropolis and still used the temple as a gathering place for birth and death, for victory and defeat, the museum industry could not have turned it into an object of tourism. We might say that formerly great works of art become mere aesthetic objects when their world disintegrates. And their cannibalization by the art industry is a result, rather than the cause, of this disintegration.

## The Individual Artwork: Yusuf and Zulaykha

While I believe that only the complete illuminated manuscript can be described as a great work of art in the Heideggerian sense, that does not mean the individual miniature painting does not lend itself to the kind of phenomenological reading that Heidegger undertakes with the work of Van Gogh, or Merleau-Ponty with that of Cézanne. Such a reading starts with a knowledge of the painting's subject matter—both literal and allegorical—just as Heidegger is not indifferent to the world of his peasant woman. But it also transcends this subject matter to arrive at the interplay of world and earth as manifested by the work of art.[9]

I will now attempt such a reading on hand of two well-known miniature paintings by the master Bihzad.[10] Since the allegorical dimensions of these works have already been analyzed by Michael Barry, I will take this analysis as a starting point for my own phenomenological reading. The first painting comes from a manuscript of the *Bustan* (Orchard), a versified story collection by the Persian poet Sadi (1210-1291/92). The volume was produced in 1488 for Bihzad's then-patron, Husayn Mirza Bayqara, Timurid ruler of Herat..[11] As pointed out by Barry, this particular painting was on display at the 1910 Munich exhibition visited by Matisse..[12]

The painting depicts Yusuf and Zulaykha, or Joseph and Potiphar's wife in the Jewish and Christian traditions. The story has been retold countless times in the Islamic tradition,.[13] but in Sadi's version as illustrated by Bihzad, "the Lady has just ordered a wizard-architect to build for her a fantastic palace with seven closed doors, within which to trap and seduce her handsome page-boy.".[14] The painting shows Yusuf, the page-boy, fleeing from Zulaykha inside the palace, and Zulaykha trying to stop him by grabbing his cloak. As Yusuf steadfastly refuses the seduction, "all seven doors fly open.".[15]

Barry introduces us to the allegorical subtext of the painting. The figures of Zulaykha and Yusuf respectively stand for the soul in search of the divine and the self-manifestation of the divine. The setting of Egypt represents the phenomenal aspect of the world. And the seven-tiered palace stands for the seven cosmic levels that must be traversed by the mystic, their doors opening to his heightened perception one by one..[16]

In terms of technique, Barry emphasizes the aspects that extend from Bihzad to Matisse, namely color and perspective. He stresses the bright, uniform colors that dominate parts of the composition, and the two-dimensionality of Zulaykha's palace, which he describes as a "carpet-page of flat architectural ornament" and a "flat colorful expanse." Finally, he dwells on the figures of Yusuf and Zulaykha that help the viewer to convert this flatness into a "conceptual three-dimensional space."[17] Barry also draws attention to Bihzad's technique of "dual illustration": Bihzad incorporates appropriate verses by poets other than Sadi, thereby establishing multi-layered intertextual relations between Sadi, his painting, and the other poetry in question.[18]

Barry does not connect his technical analysis with his allegorical reading, but it is precisely in this connection that a phenomenological reading of the painting can begin. The painting ostensibly depicts Zulaykha in the privacy of her palace. Historically, the home has been a place of the utmost importance for Muslim women, and especially for wealthy, prestigious women such as Zulaykha. Unencumbered by male oversight, such women used the home as the base from which to build, maintain, and deploy their informal networks of power, networks that reached across all layers of society. These networks could not exist without the secluded protection of the home, a space of "eligibility and exclusion," as Leslie Peirce puts it, and of "status and honor." "Authority," Peirce continues, was "a phenomenon of the inner, often literally an interior, even residential, space the boundaries of which are guarded."[19]

Therefore, when we observe Zulaykha's palace, we observe her world in its totality, the locus on which her life depends and in which most of it is spent, the locus of her seclusion and the power that stems from it. The painting, however, turns Zulaykha's dwelling inside out, revealing its most intimate corners and its most private moments, all of which she needs to conceal in order to maintain her worldly power. While all the doors and windows are shut as per the story, all the walls are open to the beholder. They are not deployed to protect and hide but, on the contrary, to show and reveal.

The effect is one of a "total or absolute vision,"[20] a vision we could call divine in that it breaks right through the overlapping of objects, allowing nothing to remain hidden behind anything else. "God, who is everywhere," Merleau-Ponty writes, "could penetrate their hiding place and see them openly deployed."[21] The painting's absence of depth and avoidance of overlap enables precisely what Merleau-Ponty calls a "participation in a Being without restriction, first and foremost a participation in the being of space beyond every particular point of view."[22]

The simultaneous deployment of different points of view applies not only to the dimension of space, but also to that of time. The painting shows the seven chambers through which Zulaykha has chased Yusuf, guiding the eye through them with the help of strategically placed diagonals, textual signposts, and colorful focal points. Traversing this seven-layered maze, the eye comes to rest on the figures of Zulaykha and Yusuf as she tears at his robe. From here, the eye is guided further along the lines of Yusuf's body to his eventual point of escape at the top of the building. Thus, although the moment captured by the figures is a specific one, the painting puts the whole story on display in a simultaneous manner. It conveys a monolithic totality of time, with the past, present, and future merged into one, the supposed ungatherables of temporal progression gathered in a single whole.

## The Individual Artwork: Layla and Majnun

Our second painting, also by Bihzad, accompanies the story of Layla and Majnun to which I briefly alluded in my discussion of Ibn Arabi. The version of the story illustrated here is part of the *Khamseh* (Quintet), a versified collection of epic narratives by the Persian poet Nizami Ganjavi (1141-1209). The painting is part of a manuscript produced in Herat in 1454, and is preserved today in the British Library, London.[23]

Depicted is the moment when Qays, the future "Majnun" ("mad for love"), sees his beloved Layla for the first time. The two, who "already love each other from reputation, as it were by instinct,"[24] are seated in the yard of a mosque, among a group of boys and girls receiving instruction. The verses that provide the painting's context are translated by Barry as follows:

> For a while they both kept the matter well hid,
> Lest the secret be disclosed unto all.
> Yet however tight and dry the string
> Which binds up tight a pouch of musk,
> The scent so sweet betrays the musk within
> And the very breeze sensed that a lover was there:
> And uplifted the veil from her Beauty![25]

As already mentioned, the story is an allegory of the love between the soul and the divine. Layla is a feminine manifestation of the divine, and the lifting of her veil is a moment of *tajalli* (theophany) in which the divine reveals itself to the soul, here represented by Qays. Layla's unveiled face, brightly illuminated while framed by her black hair, takes us back to Ibn Arabi, who uses the concepts of darkness and femininity to illustrate the transcendent aspect of the absolute, concealed yet fertile in its potential. Even as it is concealed, the absolute is always engaged in a process of unconcealment; hence Layla's unveiling and the strife between darkness and light expressed in the interplay between Layla's dark hair and the light shining on her face.

The figures of Layla and Majnun are not the only allegorical components of the painting. The schoolmaster, in whom Barry recognizes the poet Nizami himself, serves as a Sufi sheikh initiating Qays into the mysteries of divine love. The plane tree is the Tree of Life, "an image of the entire visible universe,"[26] with its leaves symbolizing "the multiplicity of visible creation."[27] Finally, the tree's protective framing of Qays signals the young lover's incipient sainthood.

The visual strategies employed in this painting are similar to those in the previous one, opening up a total apprehension of the scene that goes far beyond the capabilities of everyday perception. Interiors do not conceal but reveal: Layla, seated in front of the prayer niche inside the mosque, is revealed in her seclusion by an absence of walls. The two lovers are connected through diagonals and vacant spots that lead the eye from one to the other, as well as through the monochromatic surface on which both are seated. The different perspectives from which we see the various fences and walls seem to mimic the perspectives we would have to assume to traverse the scene in person, and thereby combine various vantage points and successive moments into one. This simultaneity of moments also extends into the future, indicated by Qays dipping his stylus into an inkwell: "Young Qays is fated to renounce the world and become a wandering dervish, a saintly hermit, an ascetic poet."[28]

From a phenomenological perspective, the overlapping placement of Layla and the prayer niche is particularly interesting. This placement, as Barry points out, reinforces the overlap between Layla and the divine. When regarding Layla, Qays must also regard the niche, just as Muslims do when praying in a mosque. "By beholding [his beloved]," Barry therefore concludes, "Qays is actually worshipping the divine."[29] Far from creating a sense of depth and distance, the overlap between Layla and the niche creates a sense of merger and identity. In concealing part of the niche (the divine), Layla simultaneously unconceals it in her own person. "The enigma" of overlapping things, Merleau-Ponty writes, lies in "their known exteriority in their envelopment and their mutual dependence in their autonomy.".[30] Whether viewed by a phenomenologist or a Sufi, Layla and the niche are both exterior to, and dependent on, each other.

Finally, the painting offers a sublime demonstration of Merleau-Ponty's "fundamental narcissism of perception,"[31] which views perception in its totality as a universal intersubjectivity of gazes in which everything simultaneously participates as both observer and observed. In describing this total vision, Merleau-Ponty falls back on the idea of the mirror:

> Painters have often dreamed about mirrors because beneath this "mechanical trick" they recognized, as they did in the case of the "trick" of perspective, the metamorphosis of seeing and the visible that defines both our flesh and the painter's vocation. This also explains why they have so often loved to draw themselves in the act of painting (they still do—witness Matisse's drawings), adding to what they could see of things at the moment, what things could see of them..[32]

The baffling multiplicity of gazes and mirroring effects we find in this painting goes far beyond its depiction of the artist (not Bihzad himself, to be sure, but his literary alter ego Nizami). By inverting an interior space, as we discussed above, the painting displays its hidden contents as if from God's perspective. Also, by offering us this perspective, the painting turns us, its viewers, into stand-ins for the divine. Finally, by featuring Layla as the mirror of the divine, the painting gives us the divine not only as perceiver, but also as perceived. Through all these features, the painting manages to interweave multiple strands of Ibn Arabi's philosophy, from the identity between the human and the divine to the cosmos as the self-disclosure of the divine.

Another layer of mutual, "narcissistic" perception is introduced in the figures of Layla and Qays, who are positioned so as to offer virtual mirror images of each other. Here, the divine as manifested in Layla is mirrored in Qays, the soul in search of its union with the absolute. And ultimately, Qays as Layla's mirror and beholder refers back to the beholder of the painting, an individuated soul in her own right, and one in which the divine seeks to behold its mirrored reflection. One could hardly ask for a more perfect instance of Merleau-Ponty's "total or absolute vision." In his words, "Essence and existence, imaginary and real, visible and invisible—painting blurs all our categories, spreading out before us its oneiric universe of carnal essences, efficacious resemblances, muted meanings."[33]

"Once art is present," Merleau-Ponty writes, "it awakens powers that are asleep in ordinary vision, a secret preexistence."[34] It is this preexistence that miniature art can be said to awaken in conjunction with Sufi principles. Ultimately, this art was rendered illegible—and the perception it engendered impracticable—due to Western encroachment, artistic and otherwise. Merleau-Ponty would seem to come full circle in trying to regain the same kind of perception, this time through Western painting. That is why, today, his thought—and that of phenomenology in general—enables us to approach miniature art on a level long inaccessible.

When painters like Henri Matisse were inspired by the first Western exhibitions of Middle Eastern miniature art, they could hardly have imagined the full extent of what they were bringing home. But then, as Merleau-Ponty puts it, the task of painting "may require the creation of new materials or new means of expression, but it may well be realized at times by the reexamination and reuse of those already at hand."[35]

# Notes

### Chapter 1. Miniature Painting in the Middle East

[1] Michael Barry, *Figurative Art in Medieval Islam and the Riddle of Bihzad of Herat (1465-1535)*, Paris: Flammarion, 2004, 27.

[2] Stuart Cary Welch, *Persian Painting: Five Royal Safavid Manuscripts of the Sixteenth Century*, New York: G. Brazilier, 1976, 11; Barry, *Figurative Art*, 27-28.

[3] Wheeler M. Thackston, *Album Prefaces and other Documents on the History of Calligraphers and Painters*, Leiden: Brill, 2001, 4; Esra Akın-Kıvanç, *Mustafa 'Ali's* Epic Deeds of Artists, Leiden: Brill, 2011, 12-13. It should be noted, however, that "the number of sources still unpublished, and therefore not readily accessible for study, is greatly in excess of the material available in printed editions" (B. N. Zakhoder, "Introduction," in Qadi Ahmad, *Calligraphers and Painters: A Treatise by Qadi Ahmad, Son of Mir-Munshi*, trans. T. Minorsky, Washington, DC: Smithsonian Institution Freer Gallery of Art Occasional Papers, 1959, 18).

[4] Thackston, *Album Prefaces*, 6-7.

[5] The album, including Dust Mohammad's preface, is preserved in the Topkapı Museum, Istanbul, Turkey.

[6] Zakhoder, "Introduction," 8.

[7] Zakhoder, "Introduction," 14.

[8] Qadi Ahmad's work contains eight miniature paintings that have survived in various extant versions of the original manuscript (Zakhoder, "Introduction," 34-36).

[9] Qadi Ahmad, *Calligraphers and Painters*, 44.

[10] Akın-Kıvanç, *Mustafa 'Ali's*, 5-10.

[11] Akın-Kıvanç, *Mustafa 'Ali's*, 24.

[12] Akın-Kıvanç, *Mustafa 'Ali's*, 112.

[13] Zakhoder, "Introduction," 17-18, 26.

[14] Akın-Kıvanç, *Mustafa 'Ali's*, 116.

[15] Akın-Kıvanç, *Mustafa 'Ali's*, 116.

[16] See Akın-Kıvanç, *Mustafa 'Ali's*, 91, 133.

[17] As a matter of fact, even the commonly used word for "album" had Sufi connotations. As Thackston puts it, the "Persian word for album is *muraqqa*', which means 'patched' or 'patchwork.' It is also the word for a dervish's frock, which was expected to be patched to exhibit the dervish's bond to poverty" (*Album Prefaces*, vii).

[18] Qadi Ahmad, *Calligraphers and Painters*, 183-184.

[19] Qadi Ahmad, *Calligraphers and Painters*, 183.

[20] Welch, *Persian Painting*, 11.

[21] Akın-Kıvanç, *Mustafa 'Ali's*, 97.

[22] Akın-Kıvanç, *Mustafa 'Ali's*, 100.

[23] Qadi Ahmad, *Calligraphers and Painters*, 184.

[24] Barry, *Figurative Art*, 38.

[25] Barry, *Figurative Art*, 51.

[26] Akın-Kıvanç, *Mustafa 'Ali's*, 194.

[27] Akın-Kıvanç, *Mustafa 'Ali's*, 144.

[28] Akın-Kıvanç, *Mustafa 'Ali's*, 108.

[29] Akın-Kıvanç, *Mustafa 'Ali's*, 206; I have slightly amended the translation.

[30] In present-day Afghanistan.

[31] Barry, *Figurative Art*, 77.

[32] Zakhoder, "Introduction," 22; Welch, *Persian Painting*, 12.

[33] Qadi Ahmad, *Calligraphers and Painters*, 158.

[34] Akın-Kıvanç, *Mustafa 'Ali's*, 270; Qadi Ahmad, *Calligraphers and Painters*, 181-182.

[35] Qadi Ahmad, *Calligraphers and Painters*, 183.

[36] Akın-Kıvanç, *Mustafa 'Ali's*, 224.

[37] Akın-Kıvanç, *Mustafa 'Ali's*, 91.

[38] David J. Roxburgh, "Concepts of the Portrait in the Islamic Lands, c. 1300-1600," *Symposium Papers LI: Dialogues in Art History, from Mesopotamian to Modern: Readings for a New Century*, Studies in the History of Art 74, ed. Elizabeth Cropper, New Haven: Yale University Press, 2009, 127.

[39] Akın-Kıvanç, *Mustafa 'Ali's*, 273. The names listed by Akın-Kıvanç are "Bartolomeo di San Marco, Gentile Bellini, Constanzo da Ferrara, Matteo de Pasti, Paolo da Pistoja, Paolo da Ragusa, Paolo Uccello, and Pinturichio."

[40] Akın-Kıvanç, *Mustafa 'Ali's*, 273-274. According to Akın-Kıvanç, historians have not been able to ascertain the identities of the two Western masters Mustafa Ali mentions in this passage.

[41] Roxburgh, "Concepts of the Portrait," 130.

[42] Roxburgh, "Concepts of the Portrait," 132. The particularities of miniature technique will be discussed further below.

[43] Qadi Ahmad, *Calligraphers and Painters*, 95.

[44] Akın-Kıvanç, *Mustafa 'Ali's*, 205.

[45] Qadi Ahmad, *Calligraphers and Painters*, 184.

[46] Thackston, *Album Prefaces*, 15.

[47] Akın-Kıvanç, *Mustafa 'Ali's*, 274. Akın-Kıvanç identifies the latter ruler as "Suleyman III," an impossibility since the Ottoman line only featured two sultans of this name.

[48] Akın-Kıvanç, *Mustafa 'Ali's*, 101.

[49] Thackston, *Album Prefaces*, 13.

[50] Zakhoder, "Introduction," 29, 31.

[51] Akın-Kıvanç, *Mustafa 'Ali's*, 92.

[52] Zakhoder, "Introduction," 30.

[53] Akın-Kıvanç, *Mustafa 'Ali's*, 23.

[54] Akın-Kıvanç, *Mustafa 'Ali's*, 236.

## Chapter 2. Artists and Sufis

[1] Akın-Kıvanç, *Mustafa 'Ali's*, 182.

[2] Akın-Kıvanç, *Mustafa 'Ali's*, 183.

[3] Thackston, *Album Prefaces*, 15.

[4] Thackston, *Album Prefaces*, 11.

[5] Qadi Ahmad, *Calligraphers and Painters*, 48; I have slightly amended the translation.

[6] Akın-Kıvanç, *Mustafa 'Ali's*, 261.

[7] Thackston, *Album Prefaces*, 15.

[8] Qadi Ahmad, *Calligraphers and Painters*, 184.

[9] He was, at the very least, the developer of the "Ottomanized" version of the *diwani* style. See Akın-Kıvanç, *Mustafa 'Ali's*, 260.

[10] Zakhoder, "Introduction," 24.

[11] Zakhoder, "Introduction," 22.

[12] Akın-Kıvanç, *Mustafa 'Ali's*, 152. Akın-Kıvanç points out that this *hadith* was well-known to Mustafa Âlî, who used it in one of the other works he authored.

[13] Roxburgh, "Concepts of the Portrait," 119.

[14] Qadi Ahmad, *Calligraphers and Painters*, 133.

[15] Thackston, *Album Prefaces*, 11.

[16] Qadi Ahmad, *Calligraphers and Painters*, 50.

[17] Zakhoder, "Introduction," 23.

[18] Zakhoder, "Introduction," 24.

[19] Zakhoder, "Introduction," 24.

[20] Qadi Ahmad, *Calligraphers and Painters*, 144.

[21] Qadi Ahmad, *Calligraphers and Painters*, 210.

[22] Akın-Kıvanç, *Mustafa 'Ali's*, 242.

[23] Akın-Kıvanç, *Mustafa 'Ali's*, 245.

[24] Akın-Kıvanç, *Mustafa 'Ali's*, 216.

[25] Akın-Kıvanç, *Mustafa 'Ali's*, 247.

[26] Akın-Kıvanç, *Mustafa 'Ali's*, 283.

[27] Akın-Kıvanç, *Mustafa 'Ali's*, 227.

[28] Thackston, *Album Prefaces*, 7; Qadi Ahmad, *Calligraphers and Painters*, 44.

[29] Zakhoder, "Introduction," 22.

[30] Akın-Kıvanç, *Mustafa 'Ali's*, 196.

[31] Qadi Ahmad, *Calligraphers and Painters*, 52.

[32] Qadi Ahmad, *Calligraphers and Painters*, 51.

[33] Qadi Ahmad, *Calligraphers and Painters*, 122.

[34] Qadi Ahmad, *Calligraphers and Painters*, 122. By "minor religious war," Moulana Sultan Ali refers to the Sufi's war against one's own ego.

[35] Akın-Kıvanç, *Mustafa 'Ali's*, 243.

[36] Akın-Kıvanç, *Mustafa 'Ali's*, 241.

[37] Zakhoder, "Introduction," 22.

[38] Thackston, *Album Prefaces*, 13.

[39] Thackston, *Album Prefaces*, 14.

[40] Qadi Ahmad does not name Ali Ashgar, only mentioning Abd al-Aziz, the son of Khwaja Abd al-Vahhab (*Calligraphers and Painters*, 186).

[41] Akın-Kıvanç, *Mustafa 'Ali's*, 268.

[42] Akın-Kıvanç, *Mustafa 'Ali's*, 269.

[43] Akın-Kıvanç, *Mustafa 'Ali's*, 269.

[44] Akın-Kıvanç, *Mustafa 'Ali's*, 270.

[45] Akın-Kıvanç, *Mustafa 'Ali's*, 141.

[46] Qadi Ahmad, *Calligraphers and Painters*, 183.

[47] Qadi Ahmad, *Calligraphers and Painters*, 183.

[48] Akın-Kıvanç, *Mustafa 'Ali's*, 268.

[49] Qadi Ahmad, *Calligraphers and Painters*, 174. As Akın-Kıvanç points out, this emphasis on Ali ibn Abi Talib as the "patron saint" of miniature art is lacking from Mustafa Ali, even though he does connect the former to the origins of calligraphy (*Mustafa 'Ali's*, 138).

[50] Thackston, *Album Prefaces*, 11.

[51] Quoted by Priscilla Soucek in her article, "The Theory and Practice of Portraiture in the Persian Tradition," *Muqarnas* 17 (2000), 97-108, here 102.

[52] Akın-Kıvanç, *Mustafa 'Ali's*, 204.

[53] Akın-Kıvanç, *Mustafa 'Ali's*, 217. The "down" here refers to the first emergence of a youthful mustache and/or beard on the artist's face.

[54] Akın-Kıvanç, *Mustafa 'Ali's*, 178.

[55] Akın-Kıvanç, *Mustafa 'Ali's*, 182.

[56] Akın-Kıvanç, *Mustafa 'Ali's*, 87.

## Chapter 3. Ibn Arabi's Ontology

[1] Mawlana Jalaladdin Muhammad Balkhi (or Rumi) was a Sufi mystic, poet, theologian, and jurist.

[2] Jalaladdin Rumi, *The Masnawi: Book One*, trans. Jawid Mojaddedi, Oxford: Oxford University Press, 2004, 212-214.

[3] Previous Sufi philosophers and poets render the competitors' approaches in reverse: both Abu Hamid al-Ghazali (1059-1111) and Nizami Ganjavi (1141-1209) have the Greeks paint and the Chinese polish (see al-Ghazali, *Wonders of the Heart*, trans. Walter James Skellie, Petaling Jaya: Islamic Book Trust, 2007, 71-72; and Nizami, *The Sikandar Nama e Bara, or Book of Alexander the Great*, trans. Henry Wilberforce Clarke, London: W.H. Allen, 1881, 638-642, respectively). Ibn Arabi, the protagonist of this chapter, also tells a version of the story, omitting the qualifiers "Chinese" and "Greek" altogether (see Ibn Arabi, *The Alchemy of Human Happiness*, trans. Stephen Hirtenstein, Oxford: Anqa Publishing, 2017, 89-90).

[4] Ibn Arabi and Rumi are widely regarded as the two pinnacles of Sufi thought, representing its philosophical and poetical expression, respectively. As Henry Corbin puts it, the Sufi tradition "is dominated by two great figures: Ibn 'Arabi, the incomparable master of mystic theosophy, and Jalaluddin Rūmī, the [...] troubadour of that religion of love whose flame feeds on the theophanic feeling for sensuous beauty" (*Alone with the Alone: Creative Imagination in the Sufism of Ibn 'Arabī*, Princeton: Princeton University Press, 1969, 110).

Apart from its towering influence on Sufism, Ibn Arabi's thought has also been linked by R.W.J. Austin to preceding, non-Islamic mystical traditions such as Kabbalah, Gnostic Christianity, and Yoga Philosophy. Austin even mentions that "an Arabic version of a Persian translation of a Sanskrit work on Tantric Yoga has been attributed to Ibn al-'Arabi." In its own turn, Ibn Arabi's work has been posited by Austin as an influence (even if indirect) on later strands of Western religious thought and literature, such as Dante's *Divine Comedy* (see R.W.J. Austin, "Introduction," in Muhyiddin Ibn Arabi, *The Bezels of Wisdom*, trans. R.W.J. Austin, New Jersey: Paulist Press, 1980, 23, 15).

While the definite establishment of such connections awaits further scholarship, it is clear that Ibn Arabi, along with many other Sufi thinkers, was deeply influenced by the Platonic and Neoplatonic traditions. The connection between Ibn Arabi and Platonic thought has been pointed out by Titus Burckhardt, who informs us that the philosopher was also referred to as "Ibn Aflātūn" (Son of Plato) ("Preface," in Ibn Arabi, *The Bezels of Wisdom*, xiii). Various other scholars, such as R.W.J. Austin, Toshihiko Izutsu, and Michael Barry, note Ibn Arabi's proximity to the Neoplatonic tradition (see Austin, "Introduction," 22-23; Toshihiko Izutsu, *Sufism and Taoism: A Comparative Study of Key Philosophical Concepts*, Berkeley: University of California Press, 2004, 154; Barry, *Figurative Art*, 299).

[5] He is said to have composed up to 400 works (Izutsu, *Sufism and Taoism*, 3).

[6] Izutsu, *Sufism and Taoism*, 4.

[7] Ibn Arabi, *The Bezels of Wisdom*, 50.

[8] Izutsu, *Sufism and Taoism*, 11.

[9] Izutsu, *Sufism and Taoism*, 31.

[10] Austin, "Introduction," 30.

[11] Izutsu, *Sufism and Taoism*, 23. Unfortunately, the subtle distinction between *Haqq* and *Allah* is often lost in translation. Thus, *Haqq* is sometimes inconsistently rendered by Izutsu and Austin as "Reality" and "God" when translating the same passage (see Ibn Arabi, *The Bezels of Wisdom*, 52 [translation by Austin as "Reality"] and Izutsu, *Sufism and Taoism*, 32 [translation by Izutsu as "God"]). Since I am drawing on both Izutsu and Austin as commentators and translators, my usage of the two words will be somewhat interchangeable. Whether I am referring to the "Absolute Mystery" or the "Creator" should, however, be clear from the context.

[12] Ibn Arabi, *The Bezels of Wisdom*, 275.

[13] At this juncture, Izutsu notes both a similarity and a difference between Ibn Arabi and Plotinus: "Ibn 'Arabi uses the Plotinian term 'emanation' (*fayd*) as a synonym of *tajalli*. But 'emanation' here does not mean, as it does in the world-view of Plotinus, one thing overflowing from the absolute One, then another from that first thing, etc., in the form of a chain. 'Emanation', for Ibn 'Arabi, simply means that the Absolute itself appears in different, more or less concrete forms, with a different self-determination in each case" (*Sufism and Taoism*, 154).

[14] Ibn Arabi, *The Bezels of Wisdom*, 56.

[15] Ibn Arabi, *The Bezels of Wisdom*, 65.

[16] Ibn Arabi, *The Bezels of Wisdom*, 125. According to Austin, the reference to an "imagination within an imagination" should be taken to mean that Ibn Arabi regards the cosmos as a kind of "divine dream," and human perception as a smaller dream within it ("Introductory Note," in Ibn Arabi, *The Bezels of Wisdom*, 119).

[17] Ibn Arabi, *The Bezels of Wisdom*, 196-197.

[18] Ibn Arabi, *The Bezels of Wisdom*, 121.

[19] Michael Barry links Ibn Arabi's concept of the dream to the Neoplatonic influence on Sufi thought: "Sufism's well-known Neoplatonic strain, here as elsewhere, dwells on the visionary experience as a mystical rapture that yields, through night and its

attendant sleep and dreams, true perception of the realities that lie beyond daylight's veil of the waking senses" (*Figurative Art*, 299).

[20] Ibn Arabi, *The Bezels of Wisdom*, 99.

[21] As Izutsu puts it, "In Ibn 'Arabi's view, if 'reality' is an illusion, it is not a subjective illusion, but an 'objective' illusion; that is, an unreality standing on a firm ontological basis. And this is tantamount to saying that it is not an illusion at all, at least in the sense in which the word is commonly taken" (*Sufism and Taoism*, 11).

[22] Izutsu, *Sufism and Taoism*, 32. The *hadith* is highly reminiscent of Friedrich Nietzsche's remarks in *The Birth of Tragedy*: "The Greeks knew the terrors and horrors of existence, but they covered them with a veil in order to be able to live" (*The Birth of Tragedy*, trans. Ronald Speirs, Cambridge: Cambridge University Press, 2014, 124).

[23] Translation by Izutsu, *Sufism and Taoism*, 75-76.

[24] As we shall see further below, a similar thought is expressed by Martin Heidegger in "The Origin of the Work of Art": "Truth is present only as the strife between clearing and concealing in the opposition between world and earth" ("The Origin of the Work of Art," in *Off the Beaten Track*, trans. and ed. Julian Young and Kenneth Haynes, Cambridge: Cambridge University Press, 2002, 1-56, here 37).

[25] Ibn Arabi, *The Bezels of Wisdom*, 50.

[26] Ibn Arabi, *The Bezels of Wisdom*, 51.

[27] Ibn Arabi, *The Bezels of Wisdom*, 56.

[28] Austin, "Introductory Note," 206.

[29] Translation by Izutsu, *Sufism and Taoism*, 226.

[30] Austin, "Introductory Note," 120; Izutsu, *Sufism and Taoism*, 62.

[31] Izutsu, *Sufism and Taoism*, 222.

[32] Abd al-Razzaq Qashani (d. 1330).

[33] Izutsu, *Sufism and Taoism*, 11-12.

[34] Izutsu, *Sufism and Taoism*, 11-12.

[35] Plato's thoughts on the divided line are expressed in the *Republic*. "Do you understand these two kinds, visible and intelligible?" Socrates asks here. "Represent them, then, by a line divided into two unequal sections. Then divide each section— that of the visible kind and that of the intelligible—in the same proportion as the line." The philosopher then goes on to describe the sections of the line, as outlined in the text above (*Republic*, trans. C. D. C. Reeve, Indianapolis: Hackett, 2004, 205-206).

[36] Ibn Arabi talks of the prophet Elias as having to "descend from the realm of his intellect to that of his lust until he becomes pure animal" in order to grasp the divine

169

not only in its transcendence, but also in its immanence (*The Bezels of Wisdom*, 235).

[37] "The angels were only certain faculties of that form which was the form of the Cosmos," Ibn Arabi states. They "do not enjoy the comprehensiveness of Adam and comprehend only those Divine Names peculiar to them" (*The Bezels of Wisdom*, 51-52).

[38] As an example of a Sufi prayer ritual (*dhikr*, literally "remembrance" of God) that emphasizes the body, we could list the whirling of the Mawlawi dervish order, established by Rumi's followers, a ritual still practiced today. Through their bodies, the dervishes free their minds; through the union of mind and body, they aim at achieving mystical union with the universe. Once again, one is reminded of Nietzsche and *The Birth of Tragedy*: "In the Dionysiac dithyramb man is stimulated to the highest intensification of his symbolic powers; something that he has never felt before urgently demands to be expressed: the destruction of the veil of maya, one-ness as the genius of humankind, indeed of nature itself" (*The Birth of Tragedy*, 21).

[39] Ibn Arabi, *The Bezels of Wisdom*, 150.

[40] Translation by Izutsu, *Sufism and Taoism*, 258.

[41] Izutsu, *Sufism and Taoism*, 44, 251, 266.

[42] Izutsu, *Sufism and Taoism*, 247.

[43] Austin reminds us that "Ibn al-'Arabī was not thinking of the specially coated glass mirrors of our day, but rather of the highly polished metal mirror of his own time. [....] To begin with, such mirrors had to be kept polished in order to preserve their reflective qualities and, furthermore, it required great skill by the craftsman to make a perfectly flat surface" ("Introductory Note," 48).

[44] In this context, Ibn Arabi quotes a *hadith* recorded by Bukhari (LXXXI:38): "I do not hesitate in what I do as much as in taking the soul of My faithful servant. He hates death as much as I hate to hurt him; but he must meet Me" (*The Bezels of Wisdom*, 273).

[45] (Jamaladdin) Nizami, *The Story of Layla and Majnun*, trans. Rudolph Gelpke, London: Bruno Cassirer, 1977.

[46] As Rumi puts it, "The drop of knowledge which You gave before / Unite now with your ocean, please, once more!" (*The Masnavi: Book One*, 117).

[47] In Izutsu's words, "Each single thing is in itself a unique existent, and yet it is immersed in the limitless ocean of Life together with all the other existents. In the first aspect, everything is unique and single, but in the second aspect, everything loses its identity in the midst of the 'water' that flows through all" (*Sufism and Taoism*, 149).

[48] "As for the philosopher," Plato maintains, "what do you suppose he thinks of the other pleasures in comparison to that of knowing where the truth lies?" (*Republic*, 282).

[49] Ibn Arabi also depicts the Gnostic ascent by referring to the heavenly spheres, a scheme developed by Gnostic thinkers and co-opted by Sufism: "The most elevated [cosmic] position is that point round which the spheres revolve, which is the Sphere of the Sun where the spiritual form of Enoch resides. There revolve round it seven higher Spheres and Seven lower Spheres, being fifteen in all" (*The Bezels of Wisdom*, 84).

[50] Izutsu, *Sufism and Taoism*, 44.

[51] Rumi, *The Masnavi: Book One*, 90.

[52] "He said, 'and my solace was made to be in prayer', which means seeing the Beloved, which brings solace to the eye of the lover" (Ibn Arabi, *The Bezels of Wisdom*, 282).

[53] Ibn Arabi, *The Bezels of Wisdom*, 235.

[54] "By prophet I mean the bringer of Sacred Law" (Ibn Arabi, *The Bezels of Wisdom*, 66).

[55] Still, as Izutsu puts it, "Even God cannot describe himself in words without delimiting himself" (*Sufism and Taoism*, 56).

[56] Fariduddin Attar, *The Canticle of the Birds, Illustrated Through Eastern Islamic Paintings*, trans. Dick Davis and Afkham Darbandi, paintings selected and annotated by Michael Barry, ed. Diane de Selliers, Paris: Editions Diane de Selliers, 2014, 138-165.

[57] Barry, *Figurative Art*, 127-128.

[58] In Moses Maimonides' words, "As everyone is aware that it is not possible, except through negation, to achieve an apprehension of that which is in our power to apprehend and that, on the other hand, negation does not give knowledge in any respect to the true reality of the thing with regard to which the particular matter in question has been negated—all men, those of the past and those of the future, affirm clearly that God, may He be exalted, cannot be apprehended by the intellects, and that none but He Himself can apprehend what he is, and that apprehension of Him consists in the inability to attain the ultimate term in apprehending Him" (*The Guide of the Perplexed*, vol. 1, trans. Shlomo Pines, Chicago: University of Chicago Press, 1963, 139).

[59] To qualify this generalization, an important proponent of *via negativa* within Christianity is Pseudo-Dionysius the Areopagite.

[60] Ibn Arabi takes the "blasphemy" promoted in this story even further. To him, if the divine is truly to be found in every cosmic phenomenon, all ways of worshiping

the divine must be equally legitimate. Anyone who sees the world like this, the philosopher states, "would allow to every believer his belief and would recognize God in every form and in every belief" (*The Bezels of Wisdom*, 283).

[61] Ibn Arabi, *The Bezels of Wisdom,* 272. According to Izutsu, Ibn Arabi also sees Muhammad as the "Seal of the Prophets" in a more ontological sense that goes back to the thought of Plotinus: "Muhammad, as the Perfect Man on the cosmic level, is the first of all self-determinations (*ta'ayyunat*) of the Absolute. Theologically, it is the first 'creature' of God." In this sense, Muhammad "corresponds almost exactly to the Plotinian First Intellect" (*Sufism and Taoism*, 236-237).

[62] Izutsu, *Sufism and Taoism*, 62.

[63] Ibn Arabi, *The Bezels of Wisdom,* 150. The quoted *hadith* is Bukhari LXXXI:38.

[64] Ibn Arabi, *The Bezels of Wisdom*, 230.

[65] Ibn Arabi, *The Bezels of Wisdom*, 107.

[66] Ibn Arabi, *The Bezels of Wisdom,* 247. The idea of oneness in multiplicity finds its classic exploration in Plotinus: "So then, being together with all things, we are those: so then, we are all and one. So therefore when we look outside that on which we depend we do not know that we are one, like faces which are many on the outside but have one head inside. But if someone is able to turn around, either by himself or having his hair pulled by Athene herself, he will see God and himself and the All; at first he will not see as the All but then, when he has nowhere to set himself and limit himself and determine how far himself goes, he will stop marking himself off from all being and will come to all the All without going out anywhere, but remaining there where the All is set firm" (*Enneads VI. 1-5*, trans. A. H. Armstrong, Cambridge: Harvard University Press, 1988, 339-341).

[67] Ibn Arabi, *The Bezels of Wisdom*, 275.

[68] Ibn Arabi, *The Bezels of Wisdom*, 274.

[69] Austin, "Introduction," 28-29.

[70] Translation by Izutsu, *Sufism and Taoism*, 202.

[71] Austin, "Introductory Note," 271.

[72] Translation by Izutsu, *Sufism and Taoism*, 203.

[73] Ibn Arabi, *The Bezels of Wisdom*, 274.

[74] Ibn Arabi, *The Bezels of Wisdom,* 275. As Corbin puts it, "A mystic obtains the highest theophanic vision in contemplating the Image of feminine being, because it is in the Image of the Creative Feminine that contemplation can apprehend the highest manifestation of God, namely, creative divinity" (*Alone with the Alone*, 159).

[75] A term also employed by Izutsu (*Sufism and Taoism*, 153-154).

[76] Ibn Arabi, *The Bezels of Wisdom*, 136.

[77] Ibn Arabi, *The Bezels of Wisdom*, 87.

[78] Rumi, *The Masnavi: Book One*, 196; *The Masnavi: Book Two*, trans. Jawid Mojaddedi, Oxford: Oxford University Press, 2007, 105.

[79] Ibn Arabi, *The Bezels of Wisdom*, 257.

[80] Ibn Arabi, *The Bezels of Wisdom*, 92.

[81] Ibn Arabi, *The Bezels of Wisdom*, 51.

[82] Ibn Arabi, *The Bezels of Wisdom*, 94.

[83] Ibn Arabi, *The Bezels of Wisdom*, 95.

[84] Ibn Arabi, *The Bezels of Wisdom*, 148.

[85] Ibn Arabi, *The Bezels of Wisdom*, 246. Ibn Arabi is quoting Quran LV:29 here.

[86] Ibn Arabi, *The Bezels of Wisdom*, 246.

[87] Ibn Arabi, *The Bezels of Wisdom*, 142.

[88] Austin, "Introductory Note," 140.

[89] Ibn Arabi, *The Bezels of Wisdom*, 141.

[90] Ibn Arabi, *The Bezels of Wisdom*, 141.

[91] "Evidence of the realities indicates that the act of creation, which occurs with the breaths eternally, constitutes an imbalance in Nature that might be called a deviation or alteration. [....] Harmony and equilibrium are everywhere sought, but never achieved. We are thus denied the rule of equilibrium" (Ibn Arabi, *The Bezels of Wisdom*, 214).

[92] Ibn Arabi, *The Bezels of Wisdom*, 155.

[93] Austin elaborates that "each inhalation represents the resolution of the Cosmos into the Essence, while each exhalation represents the creation of the Cosmos" ("Introductory Note," 146).

[94] Ibn Arabi, *The Bezels of Wisdom*, 55. In Austin's words, Ibn Arabi's cosmos "is and is not, is manifest and latent, created and uncreated, is other and non-other in a timeless divine pulse, at once creative and noncreating" ("Introductory Note," 146).

### Chapter 4. Sufism and Miniature Painting

[1] Akın-Kıvanç, *Mustafa 'Ali's*, 187. Mustafa Ali talks about the "appearance" of the prominent calligrapher Khwaja Jamal al-Din Yaqut around the time "when the hegira year passed six hundred [1204-05]." He then adds, seemingly apropos of nothing, that "the death of His Excellency the great shaykh Ibn al-Arabi and the departure of Ibn al-Farid [also] took place in the first part of the seventh century." Akın-Kıvanç misinterprets this as a reference to "Ibn al-Arabi, Muhammad b. Ziyad Abu 'Abdullah (150-231/767-846), a philologist of the school of Kufa." This attribution makes no sense for two reasons: firstly, the honorific of "great shaykh"

is routinely applied to Ibn Arabi the Sufi; and secondly, the dates for Ibn Arabi the Sufi (1165-1240) fit the time frame that Mustafa Ali is talking about, while the dates for Ibn Arabi the philologist are far off.

[2] Thackston, *Album Prefaces*, 4. The passage, "I was a hidden treasure [...] I wanted to be known, so I created creation in order to be known," as well as the passage describing the pen as "the first thing God created," are based on *hadiths*.

[3] Ibn Arabi, *The Bezels of Wisdom*, 50.

[4] The archetypes, as discussed above, are based on Platonic thought, which Sufism takes as one of the departure points in its own ontology. Among our Middle Eastern sources, it is Mustafa Ali who mentions Plato directly, quoting him as stating, "Writing is the most intelligent [deed] of the mind" (Akın-Kıvanç, *Mustafa 'Ali's*, 177).

[5] Ibn Arabi, *The Bezels of Wisdom*, 177.

[6] Thackston, *Album Prefaces*, 4.

[7] Thackston, *Album Prefaces*, 14.

[8] Thackston, *Album Prefaces*, 12.

[9] Ibn Arabi, *The Bezels of Wisdom*, 272.

[10] Thackston, *Album Prefaces*, 5.

[11] Thackston, *Album Prefaces*, 6.

[12] Thackston, *Album Prefaces*, 11.

[13] Thackston, *Album Prefaces*, 12.

[14] Thackston, *Album Prefaces*, 11.

[15] Thackston, *Album Prefaces*, 11. "Hercule" has been identified by historians as the Byzantine emperor Heraclius (r. 610-641). See Roxburgh, "Concepts of the Portrait," 120.

[16] Thackston, *Album Prefaces*, 11.

[17] Thackston, *Album Prefaces*, 12.

[18] As Roxburgh puts it, "The Chest of Witnessing portraits are copies after *acheiropoieta*, 'unmade' images fashioned by God, constituted at the beginning of time and encompassing all of God's creation and its prophetic lineage" ("Concepts of the Portrait," 120).

[19] Qadi Ahmad, *Calligraphers and Painters*, 41.

[20] Qadi Ahmad, *Calligraphers and Painters*, 48.

[21] Akın-Kıvanç, *Mustafa 'Ali's*, 34.

[22] Qadi Ahmad, *Calligraphers and Painters*, 49.

[23] Akın-Kıvanç, *Mustafa 'Ali's*, 159.

[24] Qadi Ahmad, *Calligraphers and Painters*, 41. This is a quote from the Quran (III:26).

[25] Qadi Ahmad, *Calligraphers and Painters*, 41.

[26] Thackston, *Album Prefaces*, 4-5.

[27] Thackston, *Album Prefaces*, 5.

[28] Thackston, *Album Prefaces*, 4.

[29] Thackston, *Album Prefaces*, 5.

[30] Thackston, *Album Prefaces*, 5. A similar point emphasizing the humbleness of the art of painting in comparison to divine creation is made by the Mughal emperor Akbar I (r. 1556-1605): "There are many that hate painting; but such men I dislike. It appears to me as if the painter had quite peculiar means of recognizing God; for a painter in sketching anything that has life, and in devising its limbs, one after the other, must come to feel that he cannot bestow individuality on his work, and is thus forced to think of God, the giver of life, and thus will increase in knowledge" (quoted in Soucek, "The Theory and Practice," 101).

[31] Barry, *Figurative Art*, 102.

[32] Qadi Ahmad, *Calligraphers and Painters*, 111.

[33] Akın-Kıvanç, *Mustafa 'Ali's*, 169.

[34] Quoted in Akın-Kıvanç, *Mustafa 'Ali's*, 177.

[35] Thackston, *Album Prefaces*, 5.

[36] Akın-Kıvanç, *Mustafa 'Ali's*, 177-178.

[37] Qadi Ahmad, *Calligraphers and Painters*, 106.

[38] Ladan Akbarnia and Francesca Leoni, *Light of the Sufis: The Mystical Arts of Islam*, New Haven: Yale University Press, 2010, 27.

[39] Ibn Arabi, *The Bezels of Wisdom*, 235.

[40] Rumi, *The Masnavi: Book One*, 11.

[41] Rumi, *The Masnavi: Book Two*, 104.

[42] Akın-Kıvanç, *Mustafa 'Ali's*, 143. Akın-Kıvanç makes this argument to try and explain why the authors do not attempt to formulate a theory or even philosophy of art.

[43] And, we might add, from the perspective of orthodox religion, quite possibly impermissible.

[44] Akın-Kıvanç, *Mustafa 'Ali's*, 265.

[45] Qadi Ahmad, *Calligraphers and Painters*, 159.

[46] Akın-Kıvanç, *Mustafa 'Ali's*, 273.

[47] Barry, *Figurative Art*, 34.

[48] Welch, *Persian Painting*, 16.

[49] Barry, *Figurative Art*, 38.

[50] Thackston, *Album Prefaces*, 15.

[51] Akın-Kıvanç, *Mustafa 'Ali's*, 223.

[52] Akın-Kıvanç, *Mustafa 'Ali's*, 223.

[53] Barry, *Figurative Art*, 161.

[54] Qadi Ahmad, *Calligraphers and Painters*, 180. As Minorsky explains, "The reference is to the clay birds that flew away when the child Jesus threw them into the air."

[55] Qadi Ahmad, *Calligraphers and Painters*, 178-179.

[56] Hans Jonas, *The Gnostic Religion*, Boston: Beacon Press, 2001, 208.

[57] Akın-Kıvanç, *Mustafa 'Ali's*, 8.

[58] Thackston, *Album Prefaces*, 12.

[59] Thackston, *Album Prefaces*, 12.

[60] Akın-Kıvanç, *Mustafa 'Ali's*, 277.

[61] Akın-Kıvanç, *Mustafa 'Ali's*, 277.

[62] Akın-Kıvanç, *Mustafa 'Ali's*, 279; I have slightly amended the translation.

[63] Akın-Kıvanç, *Mustafa 'Ali's*, 276-277.

[64] Akın-Kıvanç, *Mustafa 'Ali's*, 279.

[65] Akın-Kıvanç, *Mustafa 'Ali's*, 280.

[66] Qadi Ahmad, *Calligraphers and Painters*, 183.

[67] Ibn Arabi, *The Bezels of Wisdom*, 247.

[68] Akın-Kıvanç, *Mustafa 'Ali's*, 280.

[69] Akın-Kıvanç, *Mustafa 'Ali's*, 280.

[70] Akın-Kıvanç, *Mustafa 'Ali's*, 280.

[71] Fariduddin Attar, *Muslim Saints and Mystics: Episodes from the* Tadhkirat al-Auliya (Memorial of the Saints) *by Farid al-Din 'Aṭṭār*, trans. A.J. Arberry, Ames: Omphaloskepsis, 2000, 360.

[72] Attar, *Muslim Saints and Mystics*, 366.

[73] Attar, *Muslim Saints and Mystics*, 366-367.

## Chapter 5. The Journey to the West

[1] Barry, *Figurative Art*, 27-28.

[2] Barry, *Figurative Art*, 28.

[3] Barry, *Figurative Art*, 28.

[4] Barry, *Figurative Art*, 37-38.

[5] Barry, *Figurative Art*, 38.

[6] Barry, *Figurative Art*, 38.

[7] Barry, *Figurative Art*, 39.

[8] Barry, *Figurative Art*, 45.

[9] Mikhail Piotrovsky, *On Islamic Art*, St. Petersburg: Slavia, 2001, 48.

[10] Roxburgh, "Concepts of the Portrait," 121.

[11] Roxburgh, "Concepts of the Portrait," 121.

[12] Roxburgh, "Concepts of the Portrait," 126.

[13] Roxburgh, "Concepts of the Portrait," 127.

[14] Roxburgh, "Concepts of the Portrait," 121-122.

[15] Roxburgh, "Concepts of the Portrait," 120.

[16] Christiane Gruber, "Between Logos (Kalima) and Light (Nur): Representations of the Prophet Muhammad in Islamic Painting," *Muqarnas* 26 (2009): 229-262, here 249.

[17] Gruber, "Between Logos," 233.

[18] Gruber, "Between Logos," 249.

[19] Gruber, "Between Logos," 233.

[20] Gruber, "Between Logos," 231.

[21] Gruber, "Between Logos," 231.

[22] Gruber, "Between Logos," 251.

[23] Gruber, "Between Logos," 240.

[24] Gruber, "Between Logos," 230.

[25] Gruber, "Between Logos," 254.

[26] Thackston, *Album Prefaces*, 11.

[27] Ibn Arabi, *The Bezels of Wisdom*, 275.

[28] Barry, *Figurative Art*, 28.

[29] Barry, *Figurative Art*, 28.

[30] Michael Barry stresses the similarity of the influence exerted by Cézanne and miniature painting on Matisse's approach to color: "Cézanne's influence truly flowered at last in 1905, when Matisse finally altogether sundered colour from naturalism [...] to seek the pure balance of strong tints, boldly stroked, within the strict aesthetic logic of their own pictorial frame. [....] But fierce colours brushed across their canvases were precisely what Matisse [...] had so violently admired in Japanese and then in Persian Islamic art" ("'Carver of Light': Matisse and the Art of Persia and Islam," in *Global Trends in Modern and Contemporary Islamic Art*, ed. Rui Oliveira Lopes et al., Lisbon: Universidade de Lisboa, 2015, 21-59, here 30).

[31] Quoted in Barry, *Figurative Art*, 29.

[32] Quoted in Barry, *Figurative Art*, 29.

[33] Barry, *Figurative Art*, 29.

[34] Quoted in Barry, *Figurative Art*, 29.

[35] Barry, "Carver of Light," 37.

[36] Barry, *Figurative Art*, 32.

[37] Barry, *Figurative Art*, 28.

[38] Barry, *Figurative Art*, 29.

[39] Barry, *Figurative Art*, 37.

[40] Welch, *Persian Painting*, 13.

[41] Barry, *Figurative Art*, 33.

[42] Barry, *Figurative Art*, 33; see also Barry, "Carver of Light," 47.

[43] Qadi Ahmad, *Calligraphers and Painters*, 175.

[44] Qadi Ahmad, *Calligraphers and Painters*, 175.

[45] Akın-Kıvanç, *Mustafa 'Ali's*, 275.

[46] Qadi Ahmad, *Calligraphers and Painters*, 48.

[47] Thackston, *Album Prefaces*, 12.

[48] Barry, *Figurative Art*, 97.

[49] Barry, *Figurative Art*, 99.

[50] Thackston, *Album Prefaces*, 12.

[51] Barry, *Figurative Art*, 99.

[52] Barry, *Figurative Art*, 101.

[53] Barry, *Figurative Art*, 97.

[54] Barry, *Figurative Art*, 97.

[55] Barry, *Figurative Art*, 102.

[56] Barry, *Figurative Art*, 112.

[57] Barry points to Izutsu's work on Sufism and Taoism, which I have cited extensively in my chapter on Ibn Arabi, for a further exploration of this equivalence (*Figurative Art*, 113).

[58] Barry, *Figurative Art*, 112.

## Chapter 6. Phenomenology and Art: Balzac, Husserl, Heidegger

[1] Gilles Deleuze, *Francis Bacon: The Logic of Sensation*, trans. Daniel W. Smith, London: Continuum, 2003, 8.

[2] Honoré de Balzac, *The Unknown Masterpiece (Le Chef-d'œuvre Inconnu) and Other Stories*, trans. Ellen Marriage, New York: Macmillan, 1901.

[3] Balzac, *The Unknown Masterpiece*, 7. The assertion that art is not an inferior copy of nature but rather a manifestation of the artist's inner voice was a central tenet of the Romantic movement that flourished in Europe particularly in the first half of the 19th century. As Hans Blumenberg puts it, with the Romantics, "art no longer points to another, exemplary being, but rather it itself is this exemplary being for the possibilities of humanity: The work of art no longer wants to mean something; rather, it wants *to be* something" ("'Imitation of Nature': Toward a Prehistory of the Idea of the Creative Being," *Qui Parle* 12:1 [Spring/Summer 2000]: 17-54, here 47). Isaiah Berlin makes a direct comparison between the Romantics' idealized hero, Ludwig van Beethoven, and Frenhofer: "Even if [the Romantic artist] is not a genius

like Beethoven, even if, like the hero of Balzac's *Le Chef-d'oeuvre inconnu,* 'The Unknown Masterpiece,' he is mad, [...] he is a man who has dedicated himself to an ideal, who has thrown away the world" (*The Roots of Romanticism*, Princeton: Princeton University Press, 1999, 15).

[4] Maurice Merleau-Ponty, "Cézanne's Doubt," in *The Merleau-Ponty Reader*, ed. Ted Toadvine and Leonard Lawlor, Evanston: Northwestern University Press, 2007, 69-84, here 77.

[5] Balzac here utilizes the historical personages of Nicolas Poussin (1594-1665), the leading exponent of the French baroque style, and Dutch portraitist Frans Pourbus the Younger (1569-1622), next to the fictional character of Frenhofer.

[6] One option Frenhofer considers is to seek a model in "Asia," or more specifically "Turkey" (Balzac, *The Unknown Masterpiece*, 23): just like Matisse and his contemporaries, Frenhofer seems to be in search of non-Western inspirations to escape the confines of Western art.

[7] Balzac, *The Unknown Masterpiece*, 28-29.

[8] Thackston, *Album Prefaces*, 12.

[9] Balzac, *The Unknown Masterpiece*, 18-19.

[10] Balzac, *The Unknown Masterpiece*, 7.

[11] Balzac, *The Unknown Masterpiece*, 8.

[12] Balzac, *The Unknown Masterpiece*, 17.

[13] Ibn Arabi, *The Bezels of Wisdom*, 247.

[14] Edmund Husserl, *Phantasy, Image Consciousness, and Memory (1898-1925)*, trans. John B. Brough, Dordrecht: Springer, 2005, 97.

[15] Martin Heidegger, *History of the Concept of Time: Prolegomena*, trans. Theodore Kisiel, Bloomington: Indiana University Press, 1985, 43.

[16] Heidegger, *History of the Concept of Time*, 43.

[17] Husserl, *Phantasy, Image Consciousness, and Memory*, 525.

[18] Rudolf Bernet, "Phenomenological and Aesthetic Epoché: Painting the Invisible Things Themselves," in *The Oxford Handbook of Contemporary Phenomenology*, ed. Dan Zahavi, Oxford: Oxford University Press, 2012, 564-582, here 565.

[19] Heidegger, *History of the Concept of Time*, 43-44.

[20] Bernet, "Phenomenological and Aesthetic," 567.

[21] Bernet, "Phenomenological and Aesthetic," 565.

[22] Bernet, "Phenomenological and Aesthetic," 567.

[23] Gruber, "Between Logos," 249.

[24] Bernet, "Phenomenological and Aesthetic," 569-570.

[25] Bernet, "Phenomenological and Aesthetic," 567.

[26] Bernet, "Phenomenological and Aesthetic," 567.

[27] Bernet, "Phenomenological and Aesthetic," 574.

[28] Bernet, "Phenomenological and Aesthetic," 570.

[29] Translation by Izutsu, *Sufism and Taoism*, 75-76.

[30] Ibn Arabi, *The Bezels of Wisdom*, 150.

[31] My dear friend and colleague Felix Ó Murchadha has pointed out to me that the phenomenological *epoché* can be viewed as more than simply a method, and that it involves an attitude of "respect" for the phenomena that allows them to be. Emphasizing the connection between Heidegger and Christian thinkers such as Martin Luther and Meister Eckhart, Ó Murchadha holds that while phenomenology cannot be religious or moral in the concrete sense of advancing a particular, denominational account of morals, it is nonetheless possible to trace an "inherently ethical basis" of the *epoché*.

    Two authors who are not treated in this book, but whose work develops the discussion around ethics and phenomenology, are Jean-Luc Marion (see, for instance, *In Excess: Studies of Saturated Phenomena*, trans. Robyn Horner and Vincent Berraud, New York: Fordham University Press, 2002) and Michel Henry (see, especially, *Seeing the Invisible: On Kandinsky*, trans. Scott Davidson, London: Continuum, 2009).

[32] An intriguing way of teasing out parallels between Sufism and phenomenology, and Ibn Arabi and Heidegger in particular, would be via the Chinese philosophical tradition of Taoism. Izutsu's *Sufism and Taoism* offers a careful comparison of the two traditions, with particular attention to Ibn Arabi. At the same time, the connection between Taoism and Heideggerian thought has been widely discussed; see, for instance, Otto Pöggeler, "West-East Dialogue: Heidegger and Lao-tzu," in *Heidegger and Asian Thought*, ed. Graham Parkes, Honolulu: University of Hawaii Press, 1987, 47-78, and Reinhard May, *Heidegger's Hidden Sources: East Asian Influences on His Work*, trans. Graham Parkes, London: Routledge, 1996. I would very much like to try my hand at such a project in the future, ideally in collaboration with a scholar of Chinese philosophy.

[33] Ibn Arabi, *The Bezels of Wisdom*, 150.

[34] Heidegger, "The Origin," 19.

[35] Heidegger, "The Origin," 3.

[36] Mark Sinclair, *Heidegger, Aristotle and the Work of Art: Poiesis in Being*, New York: Palgrave Macmillan, 2006, 169.

[37] Heidegger, "The Origin," 6.

[38] Heidegger's hermeneutic approach to the translation of philosophical concepts from Greek into Latin falls outside the scope of this inquiry. As Karsten Harries puts it, Heidegger criticized "the translation of Greek terms into Latin" as leading to "the

rootlessness of Western thought." (*Art Matters: A Critical Commentary on Heidegger's "The Origin of the Work of Art,"* Dordrecht: Springer, 2009, 99).

[39] Heidegger, "The Origin," 6.

[40] Joseph J. Kockelmans, *Heidegger on Art and Art Works*, Dordrecht: Martinus Nijhoff Publishers, 1985, 113.

[41] Heidegger, "The Origin," 5.

[42] Heidegger, "The Origin," 7-8.

[43] Heidegger, "The Origin," 8.

[44] Martin Heidegger, *Nietzsche, Volumes One and Two*, trans. David Farrell Krell, New York: Harper & Row, 1979, 79.

[45] Martin Heidegger, *What Is Called Thinking?*, trans. J.G. Gray, New York: Harper & Row, 1968, 128.

[46] Iain Thomson points out that the term *aesthetics* "was coined by Alexander Baumgarten in the 1750s and then critically appropriated by Kant in his *Critique of Judgement* (published in 1790)" (*Heidegger, Art and Postmodernity*, Cambridge: Cambridge University Press, 2011, 47).

[47] Harries, *Art Matters*, 6-7. A philosopher similarly dissatisfied with aesthetics is Friedrich Schlegel: "In the sense in which it has been defined and used in Germany, aesthetics is a word that notoriously reveals an equally perfect ignorance of the thing and of the language. Why is it still used?" ("From *Critical Fragments*," in *Art in Theory 1648-1815*, ed. Charles Harrison et al., Oxford: Blackwell, 2000, 900).

[48] Heidegger, *Nietzsche*, 79.

[49] As Thomson puts it, "Of course, the subject/object dichotomy forms the very basis of the modern worldview, so we would be surprised if modern aesthetics did not presuppose it" (*Heidegger, Art and Postmodernity*, 48).

[50] Heidegger, *Nietzsche*, 78.

[51] Harries, *Art Matters*, 58.

[52] Ibn Arabi, *The Bezels of Wisdom*, 107.

[53] Kockelmans, *Heidegger on Art*, 5-6.

[54] Heidegger, "The Origin," 55.

[55] In this, Heidegger would seem to echo Schlegel's statement that "It is thoughtless and immodest presumption to want to learn something about art from philosophy" ("From *Critical Fragments*," 903). I strongly disagree with Steven Crowell's assertion that "Like analytic aestheticians, Heidegger is concerned to tell us what makes something a work of art" ("Phenomenology and Aesthetics; or, Why Art Matters," in *Art and Phenomenology*, ed. Joseph D. Parry, London: Routledge, 2011, 41). Rather, I think that Thomson is correct when he states that, "From a strictly Heideggerian perspective, [...] any attempt to explain 'Heidegger's aesthetics' (or

'anti-aesthetics') will look either malicious or misconceived, like a deliberate flaunting or else an unwitting display of ignorance concerning the basic tenets of his views on art" (*Heidegger, Art and Postmodernity*, 41-42).

[56] Heidegger discusses the limitations of the phenomenological method in his *History of the Concept of Time: Prolegomena*.

[57] Meyer Schapiro argues that the shoes in the painting belong to Van Gogh himself, a city-dweller, rather than to a peasant woman. According to Schapiro, the shoes in the painting should be seen as a self-portrait by Van Gogh, and Heidegger fails to notice this connection. Schapiro interprets Heidegger's stance as self-deception by the philosopher; to him, Heidegger is merely projecting his own imagination onto Van Gogh's painting ("The Still Life as a Personal Object – A Note on Heidegger and Van Gogh," in *The Reach of Mind: Essays in Honor of Kurt Goldstein*, ed. M. L. Simmel, New York: Springer, 1968, 203-209). However, Heidegger's very aim is to emancipate the painting from a restrictive interpretation, including an art historical perspective as practiced by Schapiro. As we shall see, to Heidegger, the real spirit of Van Gogh's painting lies in its revelation of the truth of the pair of peasant shoes.

[58] Heidegger, "The Origin," 14.

[59] Sinclair, *Heidegger, Aristotle*, 155.

[60] Martin Heidegger, *Being and Time*, trans. John Macquarrie and Edward Robinson, Oxford: Blackwell, 2001, 95.

[61] Heidegger, "The Origin," 21.

[62] Heidegger, "The Origin," 23.

[63] Heidegger, "The Origin," 14.

[64] Heidegger, "The Origin," 15.

[65] Heidegger, "The Origin," 15; Sinclair, *Heidegger, Aristotle*, 153.

[66] Harries, *Art Matters*, 87.

[67] Harries, *Art Matters*, 89-90.

[68] Akın-Kıvanç, *Mustafa 'Ali's*, 280.

[69] Qadi Ahmad, *Calligraphers and Painters*, 183.

[70] Heidegger, "The Origin," 23.

[71] Heidegger, "The Origin," 24.

[72] Sinclair, *Heidegger, Aristotle*, 142.

[73] Heidegger, "The Origin," 25.

[74] Heidegger, "The Origin," 25, emphasis mine.

[75] Heidegger, "The Origin," 25.

[76] Heidegger, *Being and Time*, 164-165. In "The Origin of the Work of Art," Heidegger calls such analytical approaches "act[s] of destruction" (25).

[77] Heidegger, "The Origin," 23.

[78] Sinclair, *Heidegger, Aristotle*, 51.

[79] Sinclair, *Heidegger, Aristotle*, 172.

[80] Sinclair, *Heidegger, Aristotle*, 181.

[81] My understanding of earth and world contrasts sharply with that of Hubert Dreyfus, who states that "Heidegger calls the way the artwork solicits the culture to make the meaning of the artwork explicit, coherent, and all encompassing, the world aspect of the work. He calls the way the artwork and its associated practices resist such explication and totalization the earth aspect" ("Heidegger's Ontology of Art," in *A Companion to Heidegger*, ed. Hubert L. Dreyfus and Mark A. Wrathall, Malden: Blackwell Publishing, 2005, 411).

[82] Kockelmans, *Heidegger on Art*, 155.

[83] Translation by Izutsu, *Sufism and Taoism*, 75-76.

[84] Ibn Arabi, *The Bezels of Wisdom*, 214.

[85] Kockelmans, *Heidegger on Art*, 155.

[86] Gruber, "Between Logos," 254.

[87] Heidegger, "The Origin," 21.

[88] Heidegger, "The Origin," 20-21.

[89] Heidegger, "The Origin," 21-22.

[90] Ibn Arabi, *The Bezels of Wisdom*, 247.

[91] Sinclair, *Heidegger, Aristotle*, 171.

[92] Heidegger, "The Origin," 20.

[93] Wassily Kandinsky, "From *Concerning the Spiritual in Art*," in *Art in Theory 1900-1990*, eds. Charles Harrison and Paul Wood, Oxford: Blackwell, 1992, 87. I would maintain that while a mere imitation of previous artistic traditions may well have the "stillborn" quality described by Kandinsky, acts of creative appropriation such as Matisse's usage of color strategies developed in miniature art can result in fortuitous, but nonetheless effective, rejuvenations of artistic principles.

[94] Sinclair, *Heidegger, Aristotle*, 6.

[95] Kockelmans, *Heidegger on Art*, 140.

[96] Heidegger, "The Origin," 50.

[97] To Heidegger, "The whole art industry, even if taken to the extreme and with everything carried out for the sake of the works themselves, reaches only as far as the object-being of the works. This, however, does not constitute their work-being" ("The Origin," 20).

[98] Has this disintegration, then, also been the fate of Van Gogh's painting itself? In modern times, an artwork does not seem to have the luxury of a slow death. Even before the strife between earth and world established by the painting has disintegrated, the art industry already extracts it from its context and reduces it to

an aesthetic object. One should also keep in mind that the world opened up by the work undergoes much more rapid change now than it did, say, in ancient Greece. The short lifespan of the work, then, reflects that of its world. Finally, the aesthetic approach was already well in place at the time Van Gogh produced his work. As Andrea Rehberg puts it, "when and how did a modern artwork such as Van Gogh's painting of the pair of shoes *ever* exist outside the compass of the art industry?" ("The World and the Work of Art," *Epoché* 14:1 (2009): 131-142, here 137).

A question that comes to mind is whether an artwork could possibly be recontextualized in a way that does not reduce it to an aesthetic object. The Hagia Irene Church in Istanbul might serve as an example. Originally constructed during the 4th century, the church was converted into an armory after the Ottoman conquest of Constantinople. At this point, one may perhaps speak of an equipmentalization of the work of art. Subsequently, in the 17th century, the church became a weapons museum, thereby arguably becoming aestheticized. Since the early 21st century, however, the church has been employed as a concert hall on account of its excellent acoustics, which might be interpreted as a recontextualization of the work of art, enabling it to establish a dwelling in the context of a new world.

[99] Heidegger, "The Origin," 14.

[100] Heidegger, "The Origin," 14.

[101] Martin Heidegger, *Introduction to Metaphysics*, trans. Gregory Fried and Richard Polt, New Haven: Yale University Press, 2000, 37-38.

[102] The Fried and Polt translation of Heidegger's question is actually "Why are there beings at all instead of nothing?" (*Introduction to Metaphysics*, 1). However, I think the translation provided above comes closer to the sense of Heidegger's original, "Warum ist iiberhaupt Seiendes und nicht vielmehr Nichts?" According to Heidegger, this question is particular to philosophy: "Philosophizing means asking: 'Why are there beings at all instead of nothing?' Actually asking this means venturing to exhaust, to question thoroughly, the inexhaustible wealth of the question, by unveiling what it demands that we question. Whenever such a venture occurs, there is philosophy" (*Introduction to Metaphysics*, 8).

[103] Heidegger, *Introduction to Metaphysics*, 30.

[104] Heidegger, *Introduction to Metaphysics*, 3.

[105] Heidegger, *Introduction to Metaphysics*, 7. Again, I have modified the translation of Heidegger's question.

[106] Ibn Arabi, *The Bezels of Wisdom*, 50.

[107] Ibn Arabi, *The Bezels of Wisdom*, 50.

[108] Heidegger, *Introduction to Metaphysics*, 23.

[109] Heidegger, *Introduction to Metaphysics*, 23.

[110] Heidegger, *Introduction to Metaphysics*, 17.

[111] Heidegger, "The Origin," 21.

[112] As Charles Guignon points out, the original meaning of *phusis* is lost even prior to the Romans: "In the thought of Plato and Aristotle, the initial burst of illumination was deformed into the rather constricted understanding of Being as 'beingness,' *ousia*. The understanding of Being as *ousia*, which appears at the 'ending' of Greek philosophy's inception, was itself transformed in Roman thought and language into the understanding of Being as 'substance'—that which 'lies under'—and this conception of Being has been passed down with minor variations on the theme, through the centuries to our own time" ("Being as Appearing: Retrieving the Greek Experience of *Phusis*," in *A Companion to Heidegger's* Introduction to Metaphysics, ed. Richard Polt and Gregory Fried, New Haven: Yale University Press, 2001, 34-56, here 35-36).

[113] Heidegger, *Introduction to Metaphysics*, 15-16.

[114] Heidegger, *Introduction to Metaphysics*, 15.

[115] Heidegger, *Introduction to Metaphysics*, 15.

[116] Heidegger, *Introduction to Metaphysics*, 107.

[117] Guignon, "Being as Appearing," 36.

[118] As he puts it, "for the Greeks, appearing belongs to Being, or, more sharply stated: that and how Being has its essence together *with* appearing" (Heidegger, *Introduction to Metaphysics*, 108).

[119] Heidegger, *Introduction to Metaphysics*, 107.

[120] Heidegger makes a distinction between appearing (*erscheinen*) and semblance (*Anschein*). Appearing is in a sense *lethe* or *lethic*, whereas semblance is *pseudos*. Still, Heidegger argues that semblance essentially belongs to truth as unconcealment. One is alerted by it. Being plays a trick on the observer through an entity that shows itself. This showing involves a hiding, a hiding of the entity's true being. (I would argue that semblance can be the result of *too much presence* as well. As Gilles Deleuze puts it in the case of photography, "it is not a figuration of what one sees, it is what modern man sees. It is dangerous not simply because it is figurative, but because it claims to reign over vision" [*Francis Bacon*, 11].) Semblance, then, is a form of appearing and simultaneously a form of hiddenness, both of which are characteristic of unconcealment. Semblance and being are not the same but they belong together in the form of a conflict, struggle, or strife. This strife cannot be settled or eliminated, and there is no unconcealment without the strife with semblance. (Heidegger also uses Sophocles' *Oedipus Rex* to illustrate the relationship between truth and semblance. Oedipus receives a third eye, the eye for

the truth, after having lost his two eyes that were for semblances [*Introduction to Metaphysics*, 112].)

[121] Heidegger further elaborates on the relationship between *aletheia* and truth in "The End of Philosophy and the Task of Thinking": "Why is *aletheia* not translated with the usual name, with the word "truth? [...] Insofar as truth is understood in the traditional 'natural' sense as the correspondence of knowledge with beings, demonstrated in beings, but also insofar as truth is interpreted as the certainty of the knowledge of Being, *aletheia*, unconcealment in the sense of opening, may not be equated with truth. Rather, *aletheia*, unconcealment thought as opening, first grants the possibility of truth" ("The End of Philosophy and the Task of Thinking," in *Basic Writings*, ed. David Farrell Krell, San Francsico: Harper San Francisco, 1977, 431-450, here 446).

[122] Heidegger, *Introduction to Metaphysics*, 107-108.

[123] Heidegger, "The Origin," 32.

[124] Fragment no. 123.

[125] Heidegger, *Introduction to Metaphysics*, 121.

[126] Ibn Arabi, *The Bezels of Wisdom*, 56.

[127] Ibn Arabi, *The Bezels of Wisdom*, 155.

[128] Heidegger, "The Origin," 33.

[129] Heidegger, "The Origin," 17.

[130] Gruber, "Between Logos," 233.

[131] Heidegger, "The Origin," 32.

[132] Heidegger, "The Origin," 15.

[133] Martin Heidegger, *The Question Concerning Technology and Other Essays*, trans. William Lovitt, New York: Harper & Row, 1977, 134.

[134] In Guignon's phrasing, "We tend to see the world as a collection of objects on hand for our knowing and manipulation, and we even begin to see ourselves as 'human resources' to be mobilized in the project of mastering the earth" ("Being as Appearing," 35).

[135] "Biz" (Us), in Özdemir Asaf, *Çiçek Senfonisi – Toplu Şiirler*, Istanbul: Yapı Kredi Yayınları, 2008, 16, translation mine.

[136] Henri Matisse, "Notes of a Painter," in *Art in Theory 1900-1990*, ed. Charles Harrison and Paul Wood, Oxford: Blackwell, 1992, 76.

[137] Paul Klee, "From *On Modern Art*," in *Art in Theory 1900-1990*, ed. Charles Harrison and Paul Wood, Oxford: Blackwell, 1992, 344.

[138] See the story of Mir Chalama in Akın-Kıvanç, *Mustafa 'Ali's*, 241.

[139] Ibn Arabi, *The Bezels of Wisdom*, 235.

[140] Following Sophocles' *Antigone*, Heidegger describes human beings as *pantoporos-aporos*, indicating that they travel all routes rather than being restricted to a fixed one. Further, humans do not belong to one fixed place either; they move from place to place (*polis*), and therefore are *hypsipolis-apolis*. In transcending all borders and losing its natural home, the human being becomes *deinotaton*, i.e., the uncanny, or, in Heidegger's German original, *unheimlich* (literally "homeless"). To Heidegger, it is this very homelessness that allows human beings to transcend themselves (*Introduction to Metaphysics*, 155-158).

[141] Heidegger, *Introduction to Metaphysics*, 121.

[142] In this context, the Greek temple could also be seen as a monument to human beings' struggle against their finitude and death. It is in surviving the humans who built it that the Greek temple becomes such a monument.

[143] Still, an interesting contrast remains between Ibn Arabi's and Heidegger's thoughts on death, which the former regards as the final reestablishment of unity between the particular and being, while the latter regards it as the ultimate individuator. As Heidegger maintains, "Death is in every case mine" (*Being and Time*, 284). In death, there is no such thing as "being with the others." Therefore, *Dasein*'s heading for death at every instant means *Dasein*'s drawing back from everyone by way of choosing itself.

[144] Gruber, "Between Logos," 254.

[145] Ibn Arabi, *The Bezels of Wisdom*, 92.

## Chapter 7. The Artist as Phenomenologist: Merleau-Ponty and Cézanne

[1] Heidegger, "The Origin," 50.

[2] Maurice Merleau-Ponty, "Eye and Mind," in *The Merleau-Ponty Reader*, ed. Ted Toadvine and Leonard Lawlor, Evanston: Northwestern University Press, 2007, 351-379.

[3] Merleau-Ponty, "Cézanne's Doubt," 69.

[4] Merleau-Ponty, "Cézanne's Doubt," 69.

[5] Merleau-Ponty, "Cézanne's Doubt," 70.

[6] Merleau-Ponty, "Cézanne's Doubt," 70.

[7] Merleau-Ponty, "Cézanne's Doubt," 70.

[8] Merleau-Ponty, "Cézanne's Doubt," 70.

[9] Merleau-Ponty, "Cézanne's Doubt," 72. Implied here is an argument against the Impressionists, to the effect that their objects lose themselves in the overall atmosphere of the painting.

[10] Merleau-Ponty, "Eye and Mind," 356.

[11] Merleau-Ponty, "Eye and Mind," 356.

[12] Merleau-Ponty, "Cézanne's Doubt," 76.

[13] Merleau-Ponty, "Eye and Mind," 371.

[14] Quoted in Barry, *Figurative Art*, 29.

[15] Merleau-Ponty, "Cézanne's Doubt," 73.

[16] Merleau-Ponty, "Cézanne's Doubt," 73.

[17] Merleau-Ponty, "Eye and Mind," 351.

[18] Hugh J. Silverman, "Cézanne's Mirror Stage," in *The Merleau-Ponty Aesthetics Reader*, ed. Galen A. Johnson, Evanston: Northwestern University Press, 1999, 262-278, here 265.

[19] Merleau-Ponty, "Eye and Mind," 352.

[20] Merleau-Ponty, "Eye and Mind," 351.

[21] Heidegger, *Introduction to Metaphysics*, 156.

[22] Merleau-Ponty, "Eye and Mind," 352.

[23] Merleau-Ponty, "Eye and Mind," 352.

[24] Marjorie Grene, "The Aesthetic Dialogue of Sartre and Merleau-Ponty," in *The Merleau-Ponty Aesthetics Reader*, ed. Galen A. Johnson, Evanston: Northwestern University Press, 1999, 212-233, here 227.

[25] Merleau-Ponty, "Eye and Mind," 352.

[26] Merleau-Ponty, "Eye and Mind," 352.

[27] Merleau-Ponty, "Eye and Mind," 352.

[28] Merleau-Ponty, "Eye and Mind," 370-371.

[29] Merleau-Ponty, "Eye and Mind," 352.

[30] Merleau-Ponty, "Eye and Mind," 352-353.

[31] Merleau-Ponty, "Eye and Mind," 353. As Galen Johnson points out, commentators on Merleau-Ponty's work have criticized "the privilege he has steadily accorded painting over other arts," for instance, photography and film ("Structures and Painting: 'Indirect Language and the Voices of Silence,'" in *The Merleau-Ponty Aesthetics Reader*, ed. Galen A. Johnson, Evanston: Northwestern University Press, 1999, 14-35, here 21). However, since my primary objective here is to bring Sufi and Merleau-Pontian approaches to painting into dialogue with the aim of elucidating Middle Eastern miniature painting, I will not examine such critiques of Merleau-Ponty's bias.

[32] Merleau-Ponty, "Cézanne's Doubt," 77.

[33] In the final analysis, to Merleau-Ponty, language is indirect: "If we rid our minds of the idea that our language is the translation or cipher of an original text, we shall see that the idea of *complete* expression is nonsensical, and that all language is indirect or allusive—that it is if you wish silence" ("Indirect Language and the

Voices of Silence," in *The Merleau-Ponty Aesthetics Reader*, ed. Galen A. Johnson, Evanston: Northwestern University Press, 1999, 76-121, here 80).

[34] Merleau-Ponty, "Cézanne's Doubt," 76.

[35] Merleau-Ponty, "Eye and Mind," 357.

[36] Jean-François Lyotard, "Excerpts from *Discours, figure*," in *The Merleau-Ponty Aesthetics Reader*, ed. Galen A. Johnson, Evanston: Northwestern University Press, 1999, 309-323, here 312.

[37] Mikel Dufrenne, "Eye and Mind," in *The Merleau-Ponty Aesthetics Reader*, ed. Galen A. Johnson, Evanston: Northwestern University Press, 1999, 256-262, here 260.

[38] Merleau-Ponty, "Cézanne's Doubt," 73.

[39] Merleau-Ponty, "Cézanne's Doubt," 77.

[40] Françoise Dastur, "World, Flesh, Vision," in *Chiasms: Merleau-Ponty's Notion of Flesh*, ed. Fred Evans and Leonard Lawlor, Albany: State University of New York Press, 2000, 23-50, here 45.

[41] Maurice Merleau-Ponty, *The Visible and the Invisible*, trans. Alphonso Lingis, Evanston: Northwestern University Press, 1968, 265. Quoted in Dastur, "World, Flesh, Vision," 45.

[42] Ibn Arabi, *The Bezels of Wisdom*, 214

[43] Ibn Arabi, *The Bezels of Wisdom*, 214. Austin elaborates that "each inhalation represents the resolution of the Cosmos into the Essence, while each exhalation represents the creation of the Cosmos" ("Introductory Note," 146).

[44] Dufrenne, "Eye and Mind," 258.

[45] Merleau-Ponty, "Cézanne's Doubt," 75.

[46] Merleau-Ponty, "Cézanne's Doubt," 72.

[47] Merleau-Ponty, "Eye and Mind," 357.

[48] Merleau-Ponty, "Cézanne's Doubt," 72.

[49] Merleau-Ponty, "Cézanne's Doubt," 77. It is in the context of such a forgetting, and an apprehension of the world based on brute experience, that one needs to view Merleau-Ponty's claim that a Cézanne painting "has nothing to say to the educated person" (70). As he puts it, "Cézanne conceived a work of art which [...] is valid for everyone" (71).

[50] Merleau-Ponty, "Eye and Mind," 370.

[51] Simona Erjavec, "Maurice Merleau-Ponty: Visual Perception as a Bodily Phenomenon," *AM Journal of Art and Media Studies* 2 (December 2012): 30-39, here 38.

[52] Merleau-Ponty, "Eye and Mind," 370.

[53] Merleau-Ponty, "Cézanne's Doubt," 72.

[54] Merleau-Ponty, "Eye and Mind," 365.

[55] Dastur, "World, Flesh, Vision," 30.

[56] Jessica Wiskus, *The Rhythm of Thought: Art, Literature, and Music after Merleau-Ponty*, Chicago: The University of Chicago Press, 2013, 19.

[57] Merleau-Ponty, "Cézanne's Doubt," 74.

[58] John Sallis, "Freeing the Line," in *Merleau-Ponty at the Limits of Art, Religion, and Perception*, ed. Kascha Semonovitch and Neal DeRoo, London: Continuum, 2011, 21-30, here 22.

[59] Merleau-Ponty, "Cézanne's Doubt," 74.

[60] Merleau-Ponty, "Eye and Mind," 361.

[61] Rachel McCann, "Entwining the Body and the World: Architectural Design and Experience in the Light of 'Eye and Mind,'" in *Intertwinings: Interdisciplinary Encounters with Merleau-Ponty*, ed. Gail Weiss, Albany: State University of New York Press, 2008, 265-283, here 274.

[62] Merleau-Ponty, "Cézanne's Doubt," 78.

[63] Merleau-Ponty, "Cézanne's Doubt," 79.

[64] Qadi Ahmad, *Calligraphers and Painters*, 183-184.

[65] Heidegger, "Letter on Humanism," in *Basic Writings*, ed. David Farrell Krell, San Francisco: Harper San Francisco, 1977, 213-267, here 241-242.

[66] Ibn Arabi, *The Bezels of Wisdom*, 235.

[67] Merleau-Ponty, "Cézanne's Doubt," 76.

[68] Merleau-Ponty, "Cézanne's Doubt," 76.

[69] Merleau-Ponty, "Eye and Mind," 357.

[70] Merleau-Ponty, "Eye and Mind," 355; a process summarized by Merleau-Ponty's employment of the French term *selon*.

[71] Merleau-Ponty, "Eye and Mind," 368.

[72] "Conception," Merleau-Ponty argues, "cannot precede 'execution'" ("Cézanne's Doubt," 78).

[73] Günter Figal, "Merleau-Ponty and Cézanne on Painting," in *Merleau-Ponty at the Limits of Art, Religion, and Perception*, ed. Kascha Semonovitch and Neal DeRoo, London: Continuum, 2011, 30-41, here 35.

[74] Merleau-Ponty, "Eye and Mind," 370.

[75] Merleau-Ponty, "Eye and Mind," 370.

[76] Taylor Carman, *Merleau-Ponty*, London: Routledge, 2018, 192.

[77] Akın-Kıvanç, *Mustafa 'Ali's*, 276-277.

[78] Merleau-Ponty, "Cézanne's Doubt," 76.

[79] Merleau-Ponty, "Cézanne's Doubt," 77.

[80] Balzac, *The Unknown Masterpiece*, 11.

81 Merleau-Ponty, "Eye and Mind," 355.

82 Merleau-Ponty, "Cézanne's Doubt," 73.

83 Merleau-Ponty, "Eye and Mind," 355.

84 Merleau-Ponty, "Eye and Mind," 355.

85 Merleau-Ponty, "Eye and Mind," 356.

86 Merleau-Ponty, "Eye and Mind," 356.

87 Merleau-Ponty, "Eye and Mind," 356.

88 Trevor Perri, "Image and Ontology in Merleau-Ponty," *Continental Philosophy Review* 46:1 (April 2013): 75-97, here 77.

89 Merleau-Ponty, "Eye and Mind," 356.

90 Merleau-Ponty, "Cézanne's Doubt," 76.

91 Merleau-Ponty, "Eye and Mind," 365.

92 Ibn Arabi, *The Bezels of Wisdom*, 50.

93 Merleau-Ponty, "Eye and Mind," 353.

94 Merleau-Ponty, "Eye and Mind," 354.

95 Merleau-Ponty, *The Visible and the Invisible*, 200.

96 Dastur, "World, Flesh, Vision," 35.

97 Merleau-Ponty, "Eye and Mind," 354.

98 McCann, "Entwining the Body and the World," 273.

99 Merleau-Ponty, *The Visible and the Invisible*, 139.

100 Merleau-Ponty, *The Visible and the Invisible*, 183, quoted by Galen Johnson in "Painting, Nostalgia and Metaphysics: Merleau-Ponty's Line," *Journal of French and Francophone Philosophy* 5:1 (1993): 55-70, here 62.

101 Merleau-Ponty, *The Visible and the Invisible*, 142.

102 Merleau-Ponty, "Eye and Mind," 359.

103 Ibn Arabi, *The Bezels of Wisdom*, 107.

104 For the sake of keeping my argument concise, I will not elaborate on the treatment of the mirror in the psychoanalytic tradition, particularly in the work of Jacques Lacan.

105 Merleau-Ponty, "Eye and Mind," 359.

106 Merleau-Ponty, "Eye and Mind," 359.

107 Merleau-Ponty, "Eye and Mind," 360.

108 Quoted by Merleau-Ponty, "Eye and Mind," 360.

109 Merleau-Ponty, "Eye and Mind," 360-361.

110 Merleau-Ponty, "Eye and Mind," 362.

111 Merleau-Ponty, "Eye and Mind," 362.

112 Merleau-Ponty, "Eye and Mind," 360.

113 Merleau-Ponty, "Eye and Mind," 360.

[114] Galen A. Johnson, "Desire and Invisibility in 'Eye and Mind': Some Remarks on Merleau-Ponty's Spirituality," *Merleau-Ponty in Contemporary Perspective*, ed. Philip Burke and Jan van der Veken, Dordrecht: Springer, 1993, 85-96, here 91.

[115] Johnson, "Painting, Nostalgia and Metaphysics," 63.

[116] Merleau-Ponty, "Eye and Mind," 371.

[117] At the same time, in "Eye and Mind," Merleau-Ponty brings up the concept of *manque* (lack) (356). He speaks of a lack inherent in reality, a lack of coherence, a lack in the immediately graspable, rendering our perception incomplete, thereby prompting us to respond to this lack and incompleteness, interrogating us, as it were, to elicit a response from us, an attempt to supply that which is lacking, the lack of which we have uncovered through our own interrogation of that which is in front of us. Thus, a double interrogation takes place, going in both directions between perceiver and perceived. This is as true for the painter and that which she is trying to depict as it is for the spectator who in turn beholds the painting as a completed work of art.

[118] Merleau-Ponty, "Eye and Mind," 352.

### Conclusion: Towards a Phenomenology of Miniature Painting

[1] Barry, *Figurative Art*, 38.

[2] Barry, *Figurative Art*, 27.

[3] Heidegger, "The Origin," 24.

[4] Heidegger, "The Origin," 22.

[5] Heidegger, "The Origin," 25.

[6] Sinclair, *Heidegger, Aristotle*, 171.

[7] Heidegger, "The Origin," 21-22.

[8] Ibn Arabi, *The Bezels of Wisdom*, 247.

[9] We might compare the relationship between manuscripts and miniature paintings to that between Catholic churches and the paintings they contain. While church paintings were commissioned for specific churches, walls, and purposes, such as the depiction of key events from the gospels, many have now been decontextualized and relocated to museums and other art collections. This, however, has not stopped philosophers from engaging with these paintings, sometimes interpreting them in ways that may have shocked their original creators and beholders: one need only recall Gilles Deleuze's readings of Christ portraits and his assessment of Christian painting as having produced a "properly pictorial atheism" (Deleuze, *Francis Bacon*, 9). Another interesting parallel to be pursued, as pointed out to me by my dear friend and colleague Felix Ó Murchadha, would be with the illuminated manuscripts within the Christian tradition, especially in Ireland.

[10] I am unable to reproduce the two miniature paintings in this volume, but the reader will have no difficulties locating them online on hand of the information provided here about each of them.

[11] Barry, "Carver of Light," 42-43.

[12] Barry, "Carver of Light," 42. The painting, along with its manuscript, is preserved at the Egyptian National Library. In *Figurative Art*, Barry mentions that Western curators were well aware of Bihzad's pre-eminent stature in the history of miniature art, going as far as to dub him the "Raphael of the East"—"not because of the way Bihzad actually painted, but with respect to the major influence he enjoyed within his own cultural sphere" (35).

[13] See Gayane K. Merguerian and Afsaneh Najmabadi, "Zulaykha and Yusuf: Whose 'Best Story'?" *International Journal of Middle East Studies* 29 (1997): 485–508; and Fedwa Malti-Douglas, *Woman's Body, Woman's Word: Gender and Discourse in Arabo-Islamic Writing*, Princeton: Princeton University Press, 1991.

[14] Barry, "Carver of Light," 43.

[15] Barry, "Carver of Light," 43.

[16] Barry, "Carver of Light," 43.

[17] Barry, "Carver of Light," 43.

[18] Barry, "Carver of Light," 43-44.

[19] Leslie P. Peirce, *The Imperial Harem: Women and Sovereignty in the Ottoman Empire*, New York: Oxford University Press, 1993, 9. Peirce contrasts this Middle Eastern understanding of the interior with "dominant modern Western notions of the politically significant as 'outer' and public, and the politically marginal as 'inner' or private and domestic" (9).

[20] Merleau-Ponty, "Eye and Mind," 359.

[21] Merleau-Ponty, "Eye and Mind," 363.

[22] Merleau-Ponty, "Eye and Mind," 363.

[23] Barry, *Figurative Art*, 14. British Library, Shelfmark Or. 6810, f.106v.

[24] Barry, *Figurative Art*, 14.

[25] Barry, *Figurative Art*, 14.

[26] Barry, *Figurative Art*, 15. As Barry points out, Ibn Arabi devoted a treatise, *Shajarat-ul-Kawn* ("The Tree of Life"), to this image. In the Sufi philosopher's words: "Now I looked at the universe and its genesis, at what was caused to be and how it was set forth, and I saw that the whole universe was a tree, the root of whose light is from the seed, 'Be!'" (*The Bezels of Wisdom*, 244).

[27] Barry, *Figurative Art*, 15.

[28] Barry, *Figurative Art*, 15.

[29] Barry, *Figurative Art*, 14. As Barry explains, this point is further driven home by a Quranic inscription above the niche.

[30] Merleau-Ponty, "Eye and Mind," 369.

[31] Merleau-Ponty, "Eye and Mind," 354.

[32] Merleau-Ponty, "Eye and Mind," 359.

[33] Merleau-Ponty, "Eye and Mind," 360.

[34] Merleau-Ponty, "Eye and Mind," 370-371.

[35] Merleau-Ponty, "Eye and Mind," 371.

# Bibliography

Akbarnia, Ladan and Francesca Leoni. *Light of the Sufis: The Mystical Arts of Islam.* New Haven: Yale University Press, 2010.

Akın-Kıvanç, Esra. *Mustafa 'Ali's* Epic Deeds of Artists. Leiden: Brill, 2011.

al-Ghazali, Abu Hamid. *Wonders of the Heart.* Trans. Walter James Skellie. Petaling Jaya: Islamic Book Trust, 2007.

Asaf, Özdemir. *Çiçek Senfonisi - Toplu Şiirler.* Istanbul: Yapı Kredi Yayınları, 2008.

Attar, Fariduddin. *Muslim Saints and Mystics: Episodes from the* Tadhkirat al-Auliya (Memorial of the Saints) *by Farid al-Din 'Aṭṭār.* Trans. A.J. Arberry. Ames: Omphaloskepsis, 2000.

———. *The Canticle of the Birds, Illustrated Through Eastern Islamic Paintings.* Trans. Dick Davis and Afkham Darbandi. Paintings selected and annotated by Michael Barry. Ed. Diane de Selliers. Paris: Editions Diane de Selliers, 2014.

Austin, R.W.J. "Introduction." *The Bezels of Wisdom.* By Muhyiddin Ibn Arabi. Trans. R.W.J. Austin. New Jersey: Paulist Press, 1980. 1-45.

Balzac, Honoré de. *The Unknown Masterpiece (Le Chef-d'oeuvre Inconnu) and Other Stories.* Trans. Ellen Marriage. New York: Macmillan, 1901.

Barry, Michael. *Figurative Art in Medieval Islam and the Riddle of Bihzad of Herat (1465-1535).* Paris: Flammarion, 2004.

———. "'Carver of Light': Matisse and the Art of Persia and Islam." *Global Trends in Modern and Contemporary Islamic Art.* Ed. Rui Oliveira Lopes et al. Lisbon: Universidade de Lisboa, 2015. 21-59.

Berlin, Isaiah. *The Roots of Romanticism.* Princeton: Princeton University Press, 1999.

Bernasconi, Robert. "Heidegger's Displacement of the Concept of Art." *Encyclopedia of Aesthetics.* Vol. 2. Ed. Michael Kelly. Oxford: Oxford University Press, 1998. 377-379.

Bernet, Rudolf. "Phenomenological and Aesthetic *Epoché*: Painting the Invisible Things Themselves." *The Oxford Handbook of Contemporary Phenomenology.* Ed. Dan Zahavi. Oxford: Oxford University Press, 2012. 564-582.

Blumenberg, Hans. "'Imitation of Nature': Toward a Prehistory of the Idea of the Creative Being." *Qui Parle* 12:1 (Spring/Summer 2000): 17-54.

Burckhardt, Titus. "Preface." *The Bezels of Wisdom.* By Muhyiddin Ibn Arabi. Trans. R.W.J. Austin. New Jersey: Paulist Press, 1980. xi-xvii.

Carman, Taylor. *Merleau-Ponty.* London: Routledge, 2018.

Cézanne, Paul. *Conversations with Cézanne*. Trans. Julie Lawrence Cochran. Ed. Michael Doran. Berkeley: California University Press, 2001.

Corbin, Henry. *Alone with the Alone: Creative Imagination in the Sufism of Ibn 'Arabī*. Princeton: Princeton University Press, 1969.

Crowell, Steven. "Phenomenology and Aesthetics; or, Why Art Matters." *Art and Phenomenology*. Ed. Joseph D. Parry. London: Routledge, 2011. 31-53.

Dastur, Françoise. "Merleau-Ponty and Thinking from Within." *Merleau-Ponty in Contemporary Perspective*. Ed. Philip Burke and Jan van der Veken. Dordrecht: Springer, 1993. 23-50.

————. "World, Flesh, Vision." *Chiasms: Merleau-Ponty's Notion of Flesh*. Ed. Fred Evans and Leonard Lawlor. Albany: State University of New York Press, 2000. 23-50.

Deleuze, Gilles. *Francis Bacon: The Logic of Sensation*. Trans. Daniel W. Smith. London: Continuum, 2003.

Dreyfus, Hubert L. "Heidegger's Ontology of Art." *A Companion to Heidegger*. Ed. Hubert L. Dreyfus and Mark A. Wrathall. Malden: Blackwell, 2005. 407-420.

Dufrenne, Mikel. "Eye and Mind." *The Merleau-Ponty Aesthetics Reader: Philosophy and Painting*. Ed. Galen A. Johnson and Michael B. Smith. Evanston: Northwestern University Press, 1993. 256-262.

Erjavec, Simona. "Maurice Merleau-Ponty: Visual Perception as a Bodily Phenomenon." *AM Journal of Art and Media Studies* 2 (December 2012): 30-39.

Figal, Günter. "Merleau-Ponty and Cézanne on Painting." *Merleau Ponty at the Limits of Art, Religion, and Perception*. Ed. Kascha Semonovitch and Neal DeRoo. London: Continuum, 2011. 30-41.

Grene, Marjorie. "The Aesthetic Dialogue of Sartre and Merleau-Ponty." *The Merleau-Ponty Aesthetics Reader: Philosophy and Painting*. Ed. Galen A. Johnson and Michael B. Smith. Evanston: Northwestern University Press, 1993. 212-233.

Gruber, Christiane. "Between Logos (*Kalima*) and Light (*Nur*): Representations of the Prophet Muhammad in Islamic Painting." *Muqarnas* 26 (2009): 229-262.

Guignon, Charles. "Being as Appearing: Retrieving the Greek Experience of *Phusis*." *A Companion to Heidegger's* Introduction to Metaphysics. Ed. Richard Polt and Gregory Fried. New Haven: Yale University Press, 2001. 34-56.

Harries, Karsten. *Art Matters: A Critical Commentary on Heidegger's "The Origin of the Work of Art."* Dordrecht: Springer, 2009.

Hegel, Georg Wilhelm Friedrich. *Introductory Lectures on Aesthetics*. Trans. Bernard Bosanquet. Ed. Michael Inwood. Harmondsworth: Penguin, 1993.

Heidegger, Martin. *Being and Time*. Trans. John Macquarrie and Edward Robinson. Oxford: Blackwell, 2001.

————. *History of the Concept of Time: Prolegomena*. Trans. Theodore Kisiel. Bloomington: Indiana University Press, 1985.

————. *Introduction to Metaphysics*. Trans. Gregory Fried and Richard Polt. New Haven: Yale University Press, 2000.

————. "Letter on Humanism." *Basic Writings*. Ed. David Farrell Krell. San Francisco: Harper San Francisco, 1977. 213-267.

————. *Nietzsche, Volumes One and Two*. Trans. David Farrell Krell. New York: Harper & Row, 1979.

————. "The End of Philosophy and the Task of Thinking." *Basic Writings*. Ed. David Farrell Krell. San Francisco: Harper San Francisco, 1977. 427-450.

————. "The Origin of the Work of Art." *Off the Beaten Track*. Trans. and ed. Julian Young and Kenneth Haynes. Cambridge: Cambridge University Press, 2002. 1-57.

————. *The Question Concerning Technology and Other Essays*. Trans. William Lovitt. New York: Harper & Row, 1977.

————. *What Is Called Thinking?* Trans. J. G. Gray. New York: Harper & Row, 1968.

Henry, Michel. *Seeing the Invisible: On Kandinsky*. Trans. Scott Davidson. London: Continuum, 2009.

Husserl, Edmund. *Phantasy, Image Consciousness, and Memory (1898-1925)*. Trans. John B. Brough. Dordrecht: Springer, 2005.

Ibn Arabi, Muhyiddin. *The Alchemy of Human Happiness*. Trans. Stephen Hirtenstein. Oxford: Anqa Publishing, 2017.

————. *The Bezels of Wisdom*. Trans. R. W. J. Austin. New Jersey: Paulist Press, 1980.

Izutsu, Toshihiko. *Sufism and Taoism: A Comparative Study of Key Philosophical Concepts*. Berkeley: University of California Press, 2004.

Johnson, Galen A. "Desire and Invisibility in 'Eye and Mind': Some Remarks on Merleau-Ponty's Spirituality." *Merleau-Ponty in Contemporary Perspective*. Ed. Philip Burke and Jan van der Veken. Dordrecht: Springer, 1993. 85-96.

————. "Painting, Nostalgia and Metaphysics: Merleau-Ponty's Line." *Journal of French and Francophone Philosophy* 5:1 (1993): 55-70.

————. "Structures and Painting: 'Indirect Language and the Voices of Silence.'" *The Merleau-Ponty Aesthetics Reader: Philosophy and Painting*. Ed. Galen A. Johnson and Michael B. Smith. Evanston: Northwestern University Press, 1993. 14-35.

Jonas, Hans. *The Gnostic Religion*. Boston: Beacon Press, 2001.

Kandinsky, Wassily. "From *Concerning the Spiritual in Art*." *Art in Theory 1900-1990*. Ed. Charles Harrison and Paul Wood. Oxford: Blackwell, 1992. 86-94.

Klee, Paul. "From *On Modern Art*." *Art in Theory 1900-1990*. Ed. Charles Harrison and Paul Wood. Oxford: Blackwell, 1992. 343-350.

Kant, Immanuel. *Critique of the Power of Judgment*. Trans. Eric Matthews. Trans. and ed. Paul Guyer. Cambridge: Cambrige University Press, 2000.

Kockelmans, Joseph J. *Heidegger on Art and Art Works*. Dordrecht: Martinus Nijhoff Publishers, 1985.

Low, Douglas. *Merleau-Ponty's Last Vision*. Evanston: Northwestern University Press, 2000.

Lyotard, Jean-François. "Excerpts from *Discours, figure*." *The Merleau-Ponty Aesthetics Reader: Philosophy and Painting*. Ed. Galen A. Johnson and Michael B. Smith. Evanston: Northwestern University Press, 1993. 309-323.

Maimonides, Moses. *The Guide of the Perplexed*. Vol. 1. Trans. Shlomo Pines. Chicago: University of Chicago Press, 1963.

Malti-Douglas, Fedwa. *Woman's Body, Woman's Word: Gender and Discourse in Arabo-Islamic Writing*. Princeton: Princeton University Press, 1991.

Marion, Jean-Luc. *In Excess: Studies of Saturated Phenomena*. Trans. Robyn Horner and Vincent Berraud. New York: Fordham University Press, 2002.

Matisse, Henri. "Notes of a Painter." *Art in Theory 1900-1990*. Ed. Charles Harrison and Paul Wood. Oxford: Blackwell, 1992. 72-78.

May, Reinhard. *Heidegger's Hidden Sources: East Asian Influences on His Work*. Trans. Graham Parkes. London: Routledge, 1996.

McCann, Rachel. "Entwining the Body and the World: Architectural Design and Experience in the Light of 'Eye and Mind.'" *Intertwinings: Interdisciplinary Encounters with Merleau-Ponty*. Ed. Gail Weiss. Albany: State University of New York Press, 2008. 265-283.

Merguerian, Gayane K. and Afsaneh Najmabadi. "Zulaykha and Yusuf: Whose 'Best Story'?" *International Journal of Middle East Studies* 29:4 (November 1997): 485-508.

Merleau-Ponty, Maurice. "Cézanne's Doubt." *The Merleau-Ponty Reader*. Ed. Ted Toadvine and Leonard Lawlor. Evanston: Northwestern University Press, 2007. 69-84.

———. "Eye and Mind." *The Merleau-Ponty Reader*. Ed. Ted Toadvine and Leonard Lawlor. Evanston: Northwestern University Press, 2007. 351-379.

———. "Indirect Language and the Voices of Silence." *The Merleau-Ponty Aesthetics Reader: Philosophy and Painting*. Ed. Galen A. Johnson and Michael B. Smith. Evanston: Northwestern University Press, 1993. 76-121.

———. *The Visible and The Invisible*. Trans. Alphonso Lingis. Evanston: Northwestern University Press, 1968.

Nietzsche, Friedrich. *The Birth of Tragedy*. Trans. Ronald Speirs. Cambridge: Cambridge University Press, 2014.

Nizami Ganjavi. *The Sikandar Nama e Bara, or Book of Alexander the Great*. Trans. Henry Wilberforce Clarke. London: W.H. Allen, 1881.

———. *The Story of Layla and Majnun*. Trans. Rudolph Gelpke. London: Bruno Cassirer, 1977.

Peirce, Leslie P. *The Imperial Harem: Women and Sovereignty in the Ottoman Empire*. New York: Oxford University Press, 1993.

Perri, Trevor. "Image and Ontology in Merleau-Ponty." *Continental Philosophy Review* 46:1 (April 2013): 75-97.

Piotrovsky, Mikhail. *On Islamic Art*. St. Petersburg: Slavia, 2001.

Plato. *Republic*. Trans. C.D.C. Reeve. Indianapolis: Hackett, 2004.

Plotinus. *Enneads VI. 1-5*. Trans. A. H. Armstrong. Cambridge, MA: Harvard University Press, 1988.

Polt, Richard. "The Question of Nothing." *A Companion to Heidegger's Introduction to Metaphysics*. Ed. Richard Polt and Gregory Fried. New Haven: Yale University Press, 2001. 57-82.

Pöggeler, Otto. "West-East Dialogue: Heidegger and Lao-tzu." *Heidegger and Asian Thought*. Ed. Graham Parkes. Honolulu: University of Hawaii Press, 1987. 47-78.

Qadi Ahmad. *Calligraphers and Painters: A Treatise by Qadi Ahmad, Son of Mir-Munshi*. Trans. T. Minorsky. Washington, DC: Smithsonian Institution Freer Gallery of Art Occasional Papers, 1959.

Rehberg, Andrea. "The World and the Work of Art." *Epoché* 14:1 (2009): 131-142.

Roxburgh, David J. "Concepts of the Portrait in the Islamic Lands, c. 1300-1600." *Symposium Papers LI: Dialogues in Art History, from Mesopotamian to*

*Modern: Readings for a New Century*. Studies in the History of Art 74. Ed. Elizabeth Cropper. New Haven: Yale University Press, 2009. 118-137.

Rumi, Jalaladdin. *The Masnavi: Book One*. Trans. Jawid Mojaddedi. Oxford: Oxford University Press, 2004.

————. *The Masnavi: Book Two*. Trans. Jawid Mojaddedi. Oxford: Oxford University Press, 2007.

Sallis, John. "Freeing the Line." *Merleau-Ponty at the Limits of Art, Religion, and Perception*. Ed. Kascha Semonovitch and Neal DeRoo. London: Continuum, 2011. 21-30.

Schapiro, Meyer. "The Still Life as a Personal Object – A Note on Heidegger and Van Gogh." *The Reach of Mind: Essays in Honor of Kurt Goldstein*. Ed. M. L. Simmel. New York: Springer, 1968. 203-209.

Schlegel, Friedrich. "From *Critical Fragments*." *Art in Theory 1648-1815*. Ed. Charles Harrison et al. Oxford: Blackwell, 2000. 899-903.

Silverman, Hugh J. "Cézanne's Mirror Stage." *The Merleau-Ponty Aesthetics Reader: Philosophy and Painting*. Ed. Galen A. Johnson and Michael B. Smith. Evanston: Northwestern University Press, 1993. 262-278.

Sinclair, Mark. *Heidegger, Aristotle and the Work of Art: Poiesis in Being*. New York: Palgrave Macmillan, 2006.

Soucek, Priscilla. "The Theory and Practice of Portraiture in the Persian Tradition." *Muqarnas* 17 (2000): 97-107.

Thackston, Wheeler M. *Album Prefaces and other Documents on the History of Calligraphers and Painters*. Leiden: Brill, 2001.

Thomson, Iain D. *Heidegger, Art and Postmodernity*. Cambridge: Cambridge University Press, 2011.

Waelhens, Alphonse de. "Merleau-Ponty: Philosopher of Painting." *The Merleau-Ponty Aesthetics Reader: Philosophy and Painting*. Ed. Galen A. Johnson and Michael B. Smith. Evanston: Northwestern University Press, 1993. 174-192.

Welch, Stuart Cary. *Persian Painting: Five Royal Safavid Manuscripts of the Sixteenth Century*. New York: G. Brazilier, 1976.

Wiskus, Jessica. *The Rhythm of Thought: Art, Literature, and Music after Merleau-Ponty*. Chicago: The University of Chicago Press, 2013.

Zakhoder, Boris N. "Introduction." *Calligraphers and Painters: A Treatise by Qadi Ahmad, Son of Mir-Munshi*. By Qadi Ahmad. Washington, DC: Smithsonian Institution Freer Gallery of Art Occasional Papers, 1959. 1-41.

Printed in the USA
CPSIA information can be obtained
at www.ICGtesting.com
LVHW021127290124
770086LV00009B/139

9 782494 635036